# Nassau's Historic Landmarks

Gail Saunders and Linda M. Huber

CARIBBEAN

Macmillan Education
Between Towns Road, Oxford OX4 3PP
A division of Macmillan Publishers Limited
Companies and representatives throughout the world

ISBN 0 333 79184 3

First published 2001

Photographs and cover photographs by Linda M. Huber
Etchings from Harper's *New Monthly Magazine*, Vol.XLIX, 1 Nov. 1874
Maps by Tech Type

www.macmillan-caribbean.com

Printed and bound in Thailand

2008 2007 2006 2005 2004
10 9 8 7 6 5 4 3 2

# Contents

Map of The Bahamas and inset of New Providence Island     v
Plan of Nassau     vi-vii
Introduction     viii
The historical development of the 'City of Nassau'     1

| | | | |
|---|---|---|---|
| 1 Public Square | 17 | 19 Queen Street | 70 |
| 2 Adjoining area | 20 | 20 West Street | 73 |
| 3 Bay Street | 22 | 21 Virginia Street | 75 |
| 4 West Bay Street | 28 | 22 Delancey Street | 77 |
| 5 Shirley Street | 29 | 23 Blue Hill Road | 78 |
| 6 East Bay Street | 34 | 24 Meeting Street | 80 |
| 7 East Hill Street | 39 | 25 Elizabeth Avenue | 82 |
| 8 Government House | 41 | 26 Victoria Avenue | 83 |
| 9 West Hill Street | 42 | 27 Dowdeswell Street | 84 |
| 10 East Street | 47 | 28 Fortifications and | |
| 11 Parliament Street | 51 | their environments | 88 |
| 12 Charlotte Street | 52 | 29 Nassau harbour | 92 |
| 13 Frederick Street, Prince's | | 30 Paradise Island | 95 |
| and Duke Streets | 55 | 31 Oakes Field | 97 |
| 14 Market Street | 59 | 32 Outskirts and Fox Hill | 98 |
| 15 George Street | 62 | 33 Gambier and Adelaide | 100 |
| 16 Marlborough Street | 66 | 34 Clifton Point | 101 |
| 17 Cumberland Street | 67 | | |
| 18 Nassau Court | 69 | | |

Bibliography     102
Index     104

# Acknowledgements

We should like to thank many people, especially the staff of the Department of Archives, Ministry of Education and Youth, the Antiquities, Monuments and Museum Corporation of The Bahamas, The Bahamas Historical Society, The Bahamas National Trust and the Ministry of Tourism, for their assistance in providing information.

Our thanks to the many residents of Nassau who assisted Linda onto rooftops and boats, kept their dogs at bay, told her stories of historic background and made her photography a very special and rewarding experience.

To our friend, Sylvia Brown, who spent countless hours patiently accompanying Linda to all corners of New Providence ... 'waiting for the sun to be in the right direction' ... we owe special thanks.

We are also grateful to our families, especially Gail's father, and husband Winston, for their patience and support.

We hope that this joint effort of a Bahamian author and a resident photographer, will portray the historical significance which led to modern day Nassau and will stimulate others to do further research into our rich heritage.

Motivated by each other's energy and enthusiasm, we were inspired to document some of Nassau's historic landmarks.

Gail Saunders
Linda M. Huber
February 2000

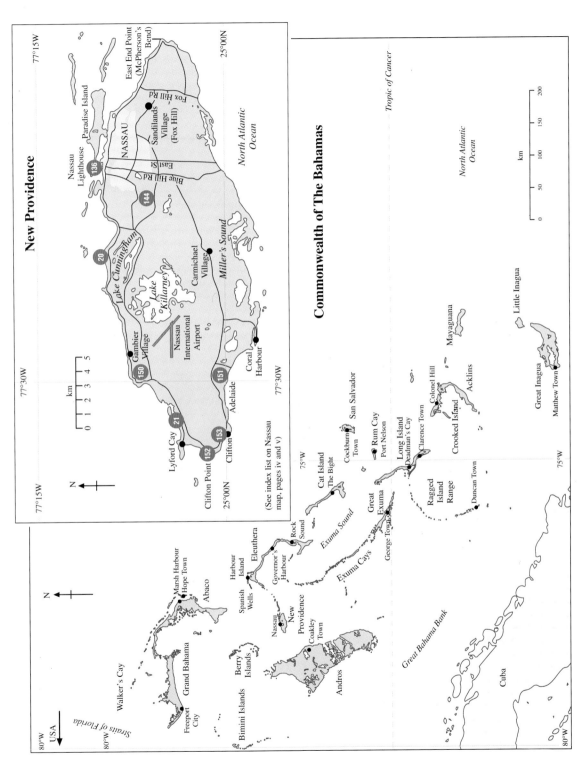

Map of The Bahamas and inset of New Providence Island

# Plan of Nassau

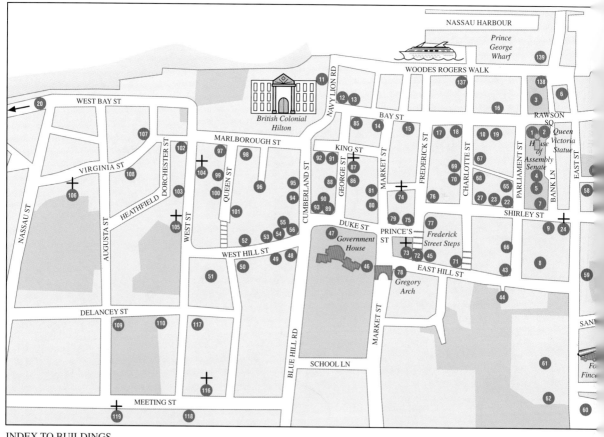

## INDEX TO BUILDINGS

**Public Square (Rawson Square)**
1 Public Buildings House of Assembly
2 Queen Victoria Statue
3 Statue of Sir Milo Butler
4 Supreme Court
5 Cenotaph
6 Churchill Building

**Adjoining area**
7 Nassau Public Library
8 Site of Royal Victoria Hotel
9 Curry House

**Bay St**
10 Masonic Building
11 British Colonial Hilton
12 Diocesan Building
13 Pompey Museum/Vendue House
14 Colombian Emeralds
15 Island Shop
16 Royal Bank of Canada
17 John Bull
18 Fendi
19 Solomon's Mines

**West Bay St**
20 Sandals Royal Bahamian Hotel
21 Old Fort

**Shirley St**
22 Magna Carta Court

23 Knowles Legal Chambers
24 Zion Baptist Church
25 Addington House
26 Princess Margaret Hospital
27 Bahamas Financial Centre
28 Tribune Building
29 Collins House
30 Bahamas Historical Society
31 St Matthew's Anglican Church
32 Ebenezer Methodist Church

**East Bay St**
33 Red Roofs
34 The Temple
35 601 Nightclub
36 Sir Milo Butler's House
37 Laurelhurst-by-the-Sea (Worrell House)
38 Toogood's Studio
39 The Pink Pearl
40 Pink Un
41 Sunnyside
42 The Hermitage

**East Hill St**
43 Jacaranda
44 Ministry of Foreign Affairs
45 Hillcrest House

**Government House**
46 Government House
47 Christopher Columbus Statue

**West Hill St**
48 Graycliff
49 West Hill House
50 Postern Gate
51 Villa Doyle
52 Ranora House
53 Sisters of Charity Convent
54 O'Donnell House
55 The Fold
56 The Corner House

**East St**
57 Cascadilla
58 H. G. Christie Ltd
59 Media House
60 Best Ever (Mortimer's) Candy Kitchen
61 Police Headquarters
62 Old Prison
63 Church of God
64 Church of God of Prophecy

**Parliament St**
65 Magistrate's Court
66 Green Shutters

**Charlotte St**
67 The Malone 'Lace' House
68 Cellar Restaurant
69 Coin of the Realm
70 Victoria Hall
71 Aurora Lodge Hall

**Frederick St/Prince's St/Duke St**
72 Frederick Street Steps
73 St Andrew's Presbyterian Church
74 Trinity Methodist Church
75 Marmaduke House
76 Rees Building
77 Apsley House and stables

**Market St**
78 Gregory Arch
79 Central Bank
80 The Balcony House
81 Verandah House
82 St Agnes Rectory
83 The Butler Residence
84 Mrs Thompson's Residence and Shop

**George St**
85 Lightbourn's Building
86 C. A. Christie Real Estate
87 Christ Church Cathedral
88 Georgeside
89 Princess House
90 Bostwick and Bostwick Chambers

**Marlborough St**
91 Pirates of Nassau
92 The Marlborough Arms

**Cumberland St**
93 Cumberland House
94 The Deanery
95 Hillside Manor

**Nassau Ct**
96 Ministry of Environment Health

**Queen St**
97 Marlborough Antiques
98 Devonshire House
99 28 Queen St
100 30 Queen St
101 Small Cottage

**West St**
102 International House
103 Yamacraw House
104 Greek Orthodox Church
105 St Francis Xavier Cathedral

**Virginia St**
106 St Mary the Virgin Angli Church
107 Dagbros
108 Christofilis Villa

**Delancey St**
109 Buena Vista
110 International Travellers Lodge

## INDEX TO BUILDINGS

Blue Hill Rd
111   St Agnes' Church
112   Grant's Town Post Office
113   Cliff's Barbershop
114   Sir Orville Turnquest's birthplace
115   Wesley Methodist Church

Meeting St
116   Bethel Baptist Church
117   The Bosfield House
118   Odd Fellows Lodge Hall
119   St John's Native Baptist Church

Elizabeth Ave
120   Lynhurst House
121   Knowles, McKay and Culmer

Victoria Ave
122   Zode House

Dowdeswell St
123   Gaylords Restaurant
124   International Tea House
125   The Smith Homestead
126   The Carey Home
127   The Duncombe Residence
128   St Matthew's Rectory and Old
        Rectory

Fortifications
129   Fort Montagu
130   Fort Charlotte
131   Fort Fincastle
132   Water Tower

133   Queen's Staircase
134   Potter's Cay Battery
135   Blackbeard's Tower

Harbour
136   Nassau Lighthouse
137   Old Nassau Ironmongery
138   Ministry of Tourism Information
        Office
139   Statue to Bahamian Women

Paradise Is
140   Atlantis
141   Grayleath
142   The Cloister

Oakes Field
143   The Nassau Guardian
144   Harry Oakes Monument
145   The College of the Bahamas

Outskirts and Fox Hill
146   The Retreat
147   St Augustine's Monastery
148   St Anne's Church
149   St Anselm's Roman Catholic Church

Gambier and Adelaide
150   St Peter's Native Baptist Church
151   St James' Anglican Church

Clifton Point
152   Wylly Plantation ruins, Clifton
153   Cut-stone steps, Clifton

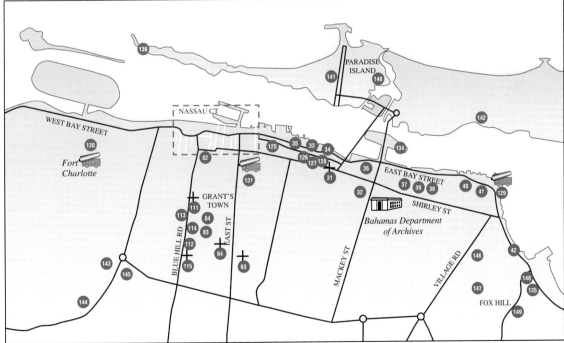

# Introduction

*Iron gates, St Andrew's Kirk*

This book complements several others written on similar themes. It attempts to capture through photography, the form and the beauty of some of the oldest and most architecturally outstanding buildings in Nassau. Unfortunately, we were unable to include all the images and information that we would have liked.

The book comprises photographs with detailed captions and brief text giving information about the major historic buildings in the town and later, the city of Nassau. It succinctly describes the major influences which shaped Nassau and concludes with a brief description of what has been achieved in the preservation and conservation of historic Nassau.

Hopefully the Antiquities, Monuments and Museum Corporation of The Bahamas, which came into force on 1 July, 1999, will build on pioneer efforts of the Department of Archives and The Bahamas National Trust in preparing a definitive Register of Historic Resources and will succeed in halting unnecessary and unwarranted demolition. The Government has also introduced measures to provide incentives to encourage owners of historic properties to preserve and conserve where possible.

This work is dedicated to all the various organizations, groups and individuals who have fought over the years and are still fighting to save 'historic Nassau'.

**Gail Saunders**
**Linda M. Huber**
February 2000

# The historical development of the 'City of Nassau'

Nassau began as a small town sometime between 1648 and 1666. Located on New Providence, originally called Sayle's Island, it was first colonized by Bermudians and English, some of whom had originally settled on Eleuthera, the 'Isle of Freedom'. By 1670 there were over three hundred settlers on New Providence. No doubt they settled at Nassau, or Charlestown, as it was called originally.

Why did Nassau become the capital city of The Bahamas and not George Town, Exuma, for instance, which also has many of the attributes of the capital? Nassau had many geographical advantages: its sheltered location, its accessibility to shipping by way of the Providence Channel and its fine harbour. In fact, its early settlers were mainly men of the sea.

The city of Nassau grew from humble beginnings. In the 1660s it comprised only a few dozens shacks. Later, in 1695, Proprietary Governor Nicholas Trott laid out Charlestown anew and renamed it Nassau in honour of the Prince of Orange-Nassau, who became William III of England. In that year, the town consisted of 160 houses. Trott also built a fort which he named Nassau. The buildings at this time were mainly wooden with thatched roofs of palmetto leaves. These small buildings were huddled around the large sheltered harbour that singled Nassau out as most suitable for the capital of The Bahamas.

During the early days the town had many ups and downs. From the late seventeenth century, privateers and pirates increasingly used Nassau as a base from which to plunder and destroy French and Spanish ships. Since the privateers were the only source of prosperity, the community and the Governor turned a blind eye on their activities. Many citizens were involved in piratical dealings. To add to its hardships, the town was attacked several times in the early eighteenth century. In 1703 it was sacked and plundered by a combined Spanish and French fleet. Being almost totally destroyed, most of the inhabitants fled. The few who stayed in Nassau 'lived scatteringly in little hutts (*sic*), ready upon any assault to secure themselves in the woods.'

Nassau's development as a modern town began in earnest under the first Royal Governor, Woodes Rogers (1718–21; 1729–32). Rogers found the town in a dilapidated state and immediately set to work to rebuild it, so that Nassau 'began to have the appearance of a civilized place.' During his second term of office, Woodes Rogers called the first General Assembly, and among the twelve Acts passed in the first session, included one 'to lay out the town of Nassau'.

Further expansion of the town took place in the 1740s during the governorship of John Tinker (1738–58) and during the 1760s under William Shirley's governorship

(1758–68). The latter Governor initiated a new survey of the town and reclaimed much of the mosquito-breeding swampland so that the town could expand eastwards. The Act of 1767 for 're-surveying of the Town of Nassau' named the 'eastern and western districts of New Providence and provided for the 'laying out and opening such streets, lanes and paths, in the Districts thereof, as may make the same more commodious and convenient to the inhabitants.' Among these new but yet unpaved streets was Shirley Street, honouring the name of the Governor who created it. Shirley Street is now the second major street to Bay Street in the city.

Notwithstanding those improvements, Nassau was still a modest town in 1783. Johann Schoepf, a German traveller who spent four months in The Bahamas on his way home from serving as a surgeon to the British forces during the Revolutionary War, portrayed Nassau as a town hugging the 'hilly shores' with houses of wood, all light and simply built. He described the town as having 'but one tolerably regular street, or line of houses, which runs next to the water'. This main road (Bay Street) was unpaved, the streets being cut down to the island's native rock. In the town, the chief houses stood apart, 'surrounded by trees, hedges and gardens'. Because of the climate, attention was given 'to roof, shade, space and air'. In the majority of cases there was simply a single planking covering the wooden house frame. 'The best are boarded double', wrote Schoepf, 'but even then the covering is light … any of our light summer houses would serve as a comfortable dwelling at Providence in all seasons.' Chimneys at Providence

*The Vendue House*

were even rarer than glass windows. The public buildings at that time comprised the 'church, a gaol and Assembly house', and *Vendue House* known as the *Bourse*, then a single-storied arcaded market building where everything was sold, including slaves and imported goods. Public notices and regulations were posted there. During the day 'buyers and sellers, ships captains and other persons of affairs or none' came to transact business or to hear or retell the latest news, or simply to gossip.

Schoepf described the inhabitants of Nassau as 'a few royal officials, diverse merchants, shipbuilders and carpenters, skippers, pilots, fishermen and what labourers are needed, with several families who live on the returns from their lands and work of their slaves'. The real planters lived on their estates in the nearby countryside. To the east of the town along the waterside were scattered houses occupied by sailors and fishermen. Several miles on, near the northern, seaside end of the present Fox Hill Village, was 'a little village, to which the name of New Guinea has been given, most of its inhabitants being free negroes and mulattoes.'

## The impact of the Loyalists

The advent of the Loyalists, who were fleeing from the newly-independent states of America in the 1780s, greatly influenced the growth of the town. Within the first decade of the arrival of the refugees new streets were built, docks and wharves were improved, a new gaol and workhouse constructed and a roofed market-place built. Architecturally, the Loyalists had a great impact on the town. The architectural styles of the Southern States and New England towns were transported to Nassau.

### Architectural changes

Besides important architectural changes brought by the Loyalists, they also ensured streets were cleaned, repaired and new ones built, and docks and wharves improved. New regulations, for example one prohibiting thatched roofs in Nassau in order to protect homeowners against fire, were passed. There was an improvement to cemeteries which were to be enclosed and a regulation passed that graves must be at least four feet deep.

The transformation of Nassau's architecture by the Loyalists stemmed from the early American influence. The American colonists before the Revolutionary War had already established their own variations of Georgian architecture. Most of the material used in the early southern colonial towns was wood. Stone was rarely used. However, in Nassau both were employed because they were readily available. In 1783 the houses in Nassau were mainly of wood and lightly built, but in the early 1800s Daniel McKinnen, a traveller, found that many houses were built of stone from local quarries, such as the one at the southern end of Elizabeth Avenue, the present site of the Queen's Staircase.

The Loyalists also patterned their houses mainly on the Georgian style, but adapted them to meet the Bahamian climate and economic conditions. Most of the houses were similar in design, consisting basically of a simple rectangular plan, two to three storeys in height, usually with an attic. The ground floor was used as a basement to house storerooms and the servants' quarters. The main rooms were at first floor level. Kitchens were usually built away from the main house so as to avoid cooking smells and excessive heat. It was also a precaution against fire.

Another characteristic aspect of the architecture of Nassau was the use of quoins. Many Loyalist buildings also incorporated large rectangular blocks of local stone. Some homes boasted delicately designed hardwood railings in a variety of patterns. Some houses had two-storeyed timber verandahs. High peaked roofs, dormer windows, brackets and lattice work were also characteristic of this period. The shipbuilding industry, active in Nassau in the late eighteenth and early nineteenth centuries, was reflected in the use of peculiar features like wooden knees or brackets which still support the balconies of *Balcony House* on Market Street north.

Not only did the Loyalists influence private architecture in the town, its suburbs and on the Out Islands but they also greatly influenced public construction. For example, Lord Dunmore, although haughty and disliked by the inhabitants of Nassau, especially the Loyalists, left a lasting legacy on the architecture of the town. His mania for building resulted in the construction of *Forts Charlotte* and *Fincastle*, and batteries at

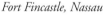

*Fort Fincastle, Nassau*

*The Nassau Public Library built between 1798 and 1800 as a prison*

Winton, Hog Island and Potter's Cay. He also built *Dunmore House*, popularly known in modern times as the *Priory*, on West Street (now demolished). For his private enjoyment he built two summer residences, the *Hermitage* on East Bay Street between 1787 and 1796, and another, now demolished, on Harbour Island, in Dunmore Town.

In 1783 the public buildings had comprised a church, a gaol and an Assembly House. Within thirty years there were at least five substantial notable new buildings, including the Public Buildings, the gaol, Government House and two churches, all with a decidedly Loyalist architectural influence.

Completed between 1805 and 1813, the *Public Buildings* were based on Governor Tryon's Palace in New Bern, the ancient capital of North Carolina. They are situated at the northern end of Parliament Street and face on to Bay Street. At the time of their construction, Rawson Square did not exist and the buildings were separated from the harbour by Bay Street.

*Nassau Public Library*, built between 1798 and 1799, was said to have been inspired by the old Powder Magazine in Williamsburg, Virginia. Its octagonal shape is unusual and it served originally as a prison.

The building of the modern *Government House* seemed to have been inspired by Loyalists as well. Situated on top of the hill known as Mount Fitzwilliam, it was completed in about 1806 and occupied shortly afterwards by Governor Cameron and his family.

### Churches

Two Nassau churches, one Anglican, the other Presbyterian, were also Loyalist inspired. *St Matthew's*, built between 1800 and 1802 to accommodate Anglicans in the eastern district of Nassau, was designed and built by Loyalist Joseph Eve, and is the oldest extant church building in Nassau. In 1823 it was considered to be at the eastern extremity of the town. It has recently been restored and its tower and spire are today important landmarks in the city of Nassau.

Another Loyalist, Michael Malcolm, was instrumental in getting the Kirk built. Its construction resulted from a plea to the St Andrew's Society, founded in 1798 in Nassau. The cornerstone of *St Andrew's Presbyterian Church* was laid in August 1810. Over the years it has undergone much renovation, but its basic Loyalist construction is still in evidence.

**Transformation of the town**

The advent of the Loyalists, who passed regulations including those for the prevention of fires, animals wandering at large and the enclosure of cemeteries, changed the appearance of the town. The shabby little port was transformed 'into a town as well built as any in the West Indies'.

# The town in 1788 and the early nineteenth century

A detailed plan of Nassau in 1788 shows that the town stretched about a mile along the waterfront and a quarter of a mile south to the parallel ridge. Within this area nearly all the streets still found between the present Victoria Avenue in the east and Augusta Street in the west, were already in existence. The town of Nassau was bounded on the west by West Street, the east by East Street, the south by East and West Streets and the north by the sea.

The downtown core, which in 1788 contained about a third of Nassau's buildings, was bounded on the north by Bay Street, which fronted on to the harbour, and to the east, south and west, by Frederick, Duke and Cumberland Streets respectively.

**Bay Street**

Bay Street, or the Strand, was the main thoroughfare, as it is now and is almost certainly the oldest street. Together with the sea and harbour, it bounds the town to the north, extends east to McPherson's Bend and to the western end of New Providence. It was the main residential and commercial street in Nassau. Most merchants had a ground floor store and lived with their family on the second storey.

The 'symbolic axis' of Nassau was George Street, which extended from Vendue House on the waterfront, past Christ Church, the sole place of worship in the city before 1802, to the Governor's House on Mount Fitzwilliam.

The better-off whites of New Providence who did not reside out of town on plantations, lived mainly in the streets just outside the commercial centre. The most substantial houses were on the crest of the ridge, originally called Hill Street but which by 1788 was known as East Hill Street and West Hill Street, being bisected by the Governor's House and Mount Fitzwilliam. Housing the elite, or *créme de la créme* of Nassau, they boasted fine architecture. While East Hill Street has lost the majority of its ancient homes to modern office buildings, West Hill Street has managed to preserve most of its historic houses. This street is architecturally pleasing and is one of the most picturesque streets in Nassau.

**East Hill Street**

The 1788 plan shows there were several residences on East Hill Street. One is believed to have been *Glenwood* which was demolished to make way for Royal Bank House. The property was owned variously by R.H. Sawyer, who had been president of the Bank of Nassau, Charles E. Bethell, President of Bethell Robertson and Company, Mrs A. Wentworth Erickson, a New Englander whose family resurrected the salt industry in Inagua, and businessman Carleton Williams. The original house is believed to have dated back to the early 1700s. Three graves were found in the garden, two are unmarked, the third belongs to Thomas Walker, Chief Justice and friend of the first Royal Governor, Woodes Rogers.

*The Hermitage, country seat of Lord Dunmore at Nassau*

Another early residence was *East Hill* originally built of cut-limestone in the early nineteenth century. It was formerly the home of the Matthews family, prominent at that time. It was briefly owned by Lord Beaverbrook. The late American businessman, S.K. Wellman of Cleveland converted it into the East Hill Club, catering mainly for professionals and high-level financial executives. It was later purchased by Carleton Williams who restored it.

Opposite Royal Bank House sits *Hillcrest* or *Bank House*, constructed in the mid-nineteenth century by Edwin Charles Moseley, founder of *The Nassau Guardian* in 1844. Hillcrest hugs the Frederick Street steps which connect East Hill Street with Frederick Street. The building was renamed *Bank House* when it became the residence of the general manager of General Finance and Banking. It was later purchased by Emanuel Alexiou and Emerick Knowles.

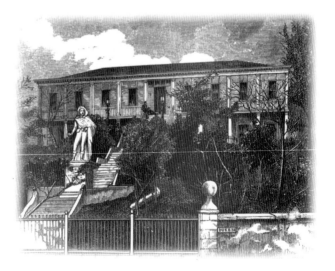

*Government House in the nineteenth century*

*Jacaranda*, a most elegant house, is said to have been built using ballast stones from Georgia in the mid-nineteenth century (c. 1840s) by Sir George Campbell Anderson, the second Bahamian to be knighted. Although remodelled, it retains much of its original structure and demonstrates the use of alternating chamfered quoins, wide latticed verandahs and traditional jalousies. The fine house, with its exceptional courtyard, has been owned by a number of people including Mr William Miller, a former Surveyor-General of the Colony, Sidney Farrington, and Captain Vyvian Drury, ADC to the Duke of Windsor (Governor of The Bahamas between 1940–5). Eunice, Lady Oakes purchased it in 1949. Mrs Shirley Oakes Butler, daughter of the late Sir Harry and Lady Oakes, acquired it and bequeathed it to her elder sister, Nancy, Baroness von Hoyningen-Huene.

The present *Government House* is constructed on the site of a much earlier house on Mount Fitzwilliam. The present building contains part of the structure built between 1803 and 1806. However, the eastern wing was badly damaged by the hurricane of 1929 and had to be demolished. The new structure to replace it was completed in 1932. The interior of Government House was lavishly redecorated in 1940 when the Duke of Windsor took up residence soon after his arrival in the colony,

*Gregory Arch* represents the gateway between Grant's Town and downtown Nassau and also links East Hill Street (west) with Government House. It was built by J. J. Burnside, Surveyor-General, who also laid out Grant's Town. Opened in January, 1852, it was named after John Gregory, Governor of The Bahamas between 1849 and 1854. The railings, imported from England, were constructed at the top of Gregory's Arch in 1854.

**West Hill Street**
Once described as the 'most beautiful street in the Caribbean', West Hill Street sits on the ridge just west of Government House. At its western end it terminates in St Francis Xavier Cathedral, while on its eastern end it leads into the main gate of Government House.

West Hill Street seemed always to have attracted royalty, celebrities and the wealthy and titled. Being built on a slope, the houses on the north side display their façades directly to the streets, while those on the south, up slope side, are set back displaying their gardens and high walls. The street is picturesque and colourful.

The buildings on West Hill Street are of limestone and local hardwood. Although architectural styles were imported mainly from the southern states, builders adapted the styles to suit the climate and economic conditions of Nassau. Many of the homes on West Hill Street have trellising and jalousies, or louvred shutters which enclose the verandahs and allow cross-ventilation. The colours used are usually pastels and complement the vegetation such as bougainvillea.

Going into West Hill Street from Government House, the first building on the left (south) is *Graycliff*, a beautifully preserved home, now a restaurant, built of stone and wood. The original building on the site is thought to have been constructed in the 1720s by Captain John Howard Graysmith, a retired pirate. It is believed that the site also contains some of the foundations of perhaps the oldest church in Nassau, which may have been destroyed by the Spaniards in 1703.

Graycliff, or Victoria House, as it was known at the time, was advertised in *The Nassau Guardian* in November 1844. Its proprietress, a Mrs Nathaniel French, offered 'Board and Lodging by the day, week or month' for Gentlemen and Ladies. The advertisement stated that 'This house is located on one of the pleasantest and most healthy situations of the town, and its accommodations are adapted as well for families or for single persons'.

Five years later its name had been changed to French's Hotel which offered 'strangers and invalids accommodations unsurpassed in The Bahamas'. It is also believed that the building served as an officer's mess for the West India Regiment. Later, Mr Polly Leach operated 'Graycliff' as a guest house and Winston Churchill and his daughter Diana were among the guests of the establishment.

The house was purchased by Canadians Walton and Dorothy Killam who lavishly refurbished it, adding a large swimming pool. The Killams sold the property to the third Earl of Staffordshire, Lord and Lady Dudley. Many celebrities and members of the Royal Family visited the Killams at Graycliff. They included Lord Beaverbrooke, Lord Mountbatten, the Duke and Duchess of Kent, the Duke and Duchess of Windsor, and Princess Alice, to name just a few. Graycliff was purchased in 1974 by Enrico Garzaroli who converted it into a five-star restaurant which is still patronized by 'the rich and the famous'.

*West Hill House* lies immediately west of Graycliff. It is believed to have been built in the mid to late nineteenth century of wood. It was once occupied by Edward St George, Chairman of the Grand Bahamas Port Authority, and at one time was owned by Sir Robert McAlpine. The present owner of Graycliff, Enrico Garzaroli purchased West Hill House in 1995 and made it his home.

*Postern Gate* lies to the west of West Hill House. The site has a complex of buildings, the main building being located right on West Hill Street. Several buildings lie to the south of the main house. The property was purchased by Enrico Garzaroli in 1997. He uses some of the smaller buildings, originally occupied by staff, for the Graycliff Cigar Factory. Postern Gate is believed to have been built in about 1840. The main building which faces West Hill Street is being renovated and turned into a factory and an exclusive 'cigar-friendly' restaurant.

Just west of Postern Gate, across Hospital Lane, is the site of a former hospital, according to the plan of 1788.

*Villa Doyle*, built in the early to mid-1860s by William Henry Doyle, is being restored to house the National Gallery of Art of The Bahamas. William Henry Doyle, a former secretary of the Educational Department, later studied law and was called to the Bahamian Bar. He became Chief Justice of The Bahamas and was knighted in 1874, being the first Bahamian to receive this honour.

Sir William Doyle, who also served as President of the Legislative Council (now Senate) was appointed Chief Justice of the Leeward Islands and later Gibraltar. He died in England in 1879. Villa Doyle was sold by his widow to William Robert Pyfrom and it changed hands several times, being owned by Walter K. Moore (later Sir Walter), the trustees of Trinity Methodist Church, Nancy Oakes, Baroness von Hoyningen-Huene, and Keith Aranha. Sir Walter Moore was responsible for the two-storey addition, in the 1920s, to the southern end of the original building. The Government purchased the building in 1994.

Villa Doyle has been described as one of 'the finest buildings in Nassau'. This spacious mansion was designed by a Mr Walsh of the Royal Engineers and is a rare example of Palladian architecture in the Caribbean. The main house is built of quarried limestone, comprising two wings joined by a partially enclosed stairway. The old section has front verandahs facing north, while the newer section has a continuous verandah on the second floor. The verandahs have carved timber railings.

*St Francis Xavier Cathedral* is believed to be the first Roman Catholic Church built in The Bahamas. It is located on top of the hill at the corner of West and West Hill Streets, opposite Villa Doyle. Its cornerstone was laid on 25 August, 1885 on land purchased from the Revd Robert Dunlop, a Presbyterian Minister. While being constructed, the church was struck by lightning and one of the workmen, Thomas Mackey, was killed. The roof, stone work and doors of the building were damaged. It was not until November 1886 that the first mass was celebrated, by the Revd J.A. Ryan of New York. St Francis Xavier Church was officially dedicated in February 1887 by Archbishop Michael Corrigan of New York.

The early days of Roman Catholicism were difficult and the congregation small. Father O'Keefe, the resident priest, became discouraged by 1889 because of the prejudice against Catholics and the lack of financial support. He left The Bahamas, returning to New York, and thus St Francis Xavier was closed, but only temporarily. The Sisters of Charity from Mount St Vincent-on-the-Hudson, New York and a Benedictine priest from St John's Abbey, Minnesota were recruited and revived Roman Catholicism in Nassau and The Bahamas. St Francis Xavier Church was elevated to the status of a Cathedral in 1960.

On the northern side of West Hill Street is *Sunningridge* which straddles the steps leading down to Queen Street. A building on the site on which it stands appears on the 1788 plan of Nassau. However, the present structure probably dates to the mid to late nineteenth century.

At the time of writing Sunningridge had been acquired by Canadian developer Jeffrey Waterous. It had been gutted with plans for restoration. It has three storeys on the street side and four on the downhill northern side. It is most attractive and boasts two enclosed jalousied verandahs, dormer windows and a tower from which there is a magnificent view of the harbour. The terraced courtyard contains an old covered well surrounded by attractive palm trees. The house was once occupied by the late land and property promoter, Sir Harold Christie and was believed to have been owned or occupied by the controversial Swedish industrialist, the late Axel Wenner-Gren, and the late Julian Maynard and his family.

The original structure on the site of *Ranora House*, dating back to the late 1860s, was probably the three-storey building which served as the rectory for St Mary the Virgin (Anglican) Church on Virginia Street. It was called St Mary's Villa at first. Following the First World War the house was sold to Sir George and Lady Johnson who retained the name, St Mary's Villa. Mrs Cora Munson, of the Munson Shipping Lines, bought the house in 1939 and renamed it Ranora House. She added the east and west wings and changed the main entrance from West Hill Street to the eastern courtyard. Ranora House changed hands a couple more times and also served as a temporary home for the Governor of Nassau, Sir Ralph Grey (1964–8). Eric and Betty Cottell, who are keen to preserve West Hill Street, now own Ranora House.

Immediately east of Ranora House is the former *Sisters of Charity Convent*. Shortly after St Francis Roman Catholic Church was consecrated, in February 1887, the Honourable Jacob Webb deeded the property on which the convent stands to Archbishop Corrigan of New York. Ten years later, in August 1897, the Archbishop deeded the property to the Sisters of Charity.

The original five sisters provided education for about 150 pupils and as late as the early 1970s, 21 nuns lived at the Convent, teaching in Roman Catholic schools. The academy, originally located at the western end of the Convent, developed into Xavier's College, now located on West Bay. The Convent was gutted by its new owner Jeffrey Waterous, but there are plans to restore it and turn it into a small art gallery and workshop area for student artists.

The *O'Donnell House,* just east of the Convent, is believed to have been constructed in the late 1800s. It was owned by a Canadian named Dalley, from about 1910 to the late 1950s. Not much is known of its early history. Columbus O'Donnell and his wife, Sibilla, (now O'Donnell-Clarke) bought the house in 1959. Mr O'Donnell's mother, Mrs John F.C. Bryce, lived nearby in Market Street, in the historic Balcony House, thought to have been built in about 1790.

The O'Donnell House was constructed of horseflesh wood, displaying a louvred verandah and a porch with wooden railing. It is a beautiful house with cultivated vines and hedges, with a swimming pool and a guest house to the east of the main house. The house is important not only because of its age and architectural style, but also for the famous personages who have visited and stayed there. The late Lord Mountbatten, a long time friend of the O'Donnells, and his family spent a few days there every year for about thirty years on their way to Windermere Island in Eleuthera, their winter retreat. Prince Charles has also been a guest of the O'Donnells. Mr Jeffrey Waterous is presently leasing it as the headquarters for his Nassau-based Mercantile Petroleum Company.

*The Fold* is an unusual building which was constructed in about 1840. It is presently being renovated.

There is a building on the 1788 plan of Nassau where the *Corner House* is located. The present building appears to be mid to late nineteenth century. It is a simple structure with thick limestone walls on the lower storey while the upper storey is of wood. It has recently been restored. Not much is known of its early history. It was once owned by a British Army captain named Meade and teacher, Ms Molly Albury, aunt of Bishop Michael Eldon and Dr Keva Bethel, former President of the College of The Bahamas.

## Over-the-Hill

Most ex-slaves and free blacks lived in the 'over-the-hill' area south of the Governor's House and slightly to the south-west in Delancey Town 'behind the hospital'. The

*Early morning in Nassau Market in the nineteenth century*

majority of blacks lived over the 'hill' or ridge that separated downtown or 'white' Nassau from the exclusively black settlements to the south. The life and culture of the black suburbs and outlying settlements were so distinct that nineteenth-century writers regarded the settlements as exotic 'native quarters'.

'Over-the-Hill' comprised Grant's Town, Bain Town and a part of Delancey Town. Grant's Town, laid out between 1820 and 1829 by Surveyor-General, John Burnside on the instruction of Governor Lewis Grant, was settled by liberated Africans and former slaves. It was bordered on the east by East Street, on the west by Blue Hill Road, on the north by Cockburn and Lees Streets, and in the south by the Blue Hills.

Bain Town is located to the west of Grant's Town. It was originally part of a 140-acre land grant to one Susannah Weatherspoon, and was sold to a black Bahamian businessman Charles H. Bain in the late 1840s. He divided the land into allotments and sold them at moderate prices to blacks – both liberated Africans and ex-slaves. It is believed that Bain Town was named in his honour. Bain Town was bordered on the west by Nassau Street, on the east by Blue Hill Road, on the north by South Street and on the south by what is now Poincianna Drive.

Delancey Town, the southern part of which can be considered Over-the-Hill, is located to the west of the town of Nassau. Located behind Dunmore House which was Government House in the late eighteenth century, it stretched from West Hill Street in the north to South Street in the south, Nassau Street in the west and Hospital Lane in the east. The area was named after Stephen Delancey, then Chief Justice of The Bahamas, who purchased 150 acres of land from a John Brown in 1789. The lots were laid out carefully as an extension to the Nassau grid, and were surveyed. Parcels were apportioned to families of slaves, some of whom were provided with modest cabins.

The three towns were separated by luxuriant foliage of bushes and trees, which were gradually cleared by the early twentieth century, thus connecting the settlements. The entire black district became known as Over-the-Hill.

**Liberated African settlements**
Other black settlements, settled by liberated Africans captured by the Royal Navy after the abolition of the slave trade in 1807, were a greater distance from Nassau. They included Adelaide and Carmichael in the south-west, and Gambier in the west.

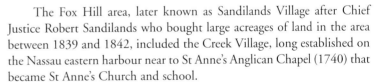

The Fox Hill area, later known as Sandilands Village after Chief Justice Robert Sandilands who bought large acreages of land in the area between 1839 and 1842, included the Creek Village, long established on the Nassau eastern harbour near to St Anne's Anglican Chapel (1740) that became St Anne's Church and school.

Sandilands Village contained four 'towns': Congo, Nango and Joshua Towns settled by liberated Africans, and Burnside Town named after the white Surveyor-General, and founded by Bahamian-born former slaves.

*Entrance to the Port of Nassau*

The majority of the houses of the black population were built mostly of wood, but some had walls of plastered limestone rubble, wattle or daub, or even in cases of dire poverty, thatched palmetto on flimsy wooden frames. They were small wooden two- to three-room houses. Roofs were usually of palmetto thatch (the making of which was an African skill), some were of native cedar shingles.

Most houses had no glass, board shutters were used instead, and fireplaces and chimneys were rare. Cooking was usually done outdoors on a small fire.

*Royal Victoria Hotel, opened in 1861*

# The mid to late nineteenth century

By the 1840s Nassau, still described as 'a sleepy town' of 8000 inhabitants, was scattered on the southern side of Bay Street and on the northern slopes of the ridge, now East Hill and West Hill Streets. The town did not extend west of West Street or east of St Matthew's Church. Between the 1840s and 1860s some fine Georgian colonial-style homes, such as Graycliff, East Hill and Jacaranda were built. These stately buildings have been well preserved. The decades of the 1840s and 1850s witnessed a slow but steady growth of Nassau.

The pace of development increased during the 1860s with the outbreak of the American Civil War. The beginning of the conflict coincided with the granting in 1861 of Letters Patent which raised Christ Church to the status of a Cathedral and the town of Nassau to the City of Nassau. The tourist industry was becoming important, being encouraged by the 1859 contract made between The Bahamas Government and Mr Samuel Cunard for a regular steamship connection between Nassau and New York. Additionally, the *Royal Victoria Hotel* was built to accommodate winter visitors. It soon became the headquarters of the colourful blockade runners. The brief prosperity brought by the war stimulated some improvements in Nassau. For the first time, Bay Street was widened and provided with kerbstones and lights. The north side of Bay Street was reclaimed and warehouses and shops built, including John S. George on the corner of East and Bay Streets. The old prison on East Street was built towards the end of the blockade period.

However, tragedy was again to strike Nassau. To add to the drastic decline in the economy in October 1866, a devastating hurricane passed over the city destroying over 600 houses and damaging many more. Among the buildings demolished was the newly-constructed Trinity Church which was, however, rebuilt three years later.

Nassau recovered slowly and by 1880 could be described as 'a nice-looking' town with 'nice wide' and clean streets 'shaded with cork and almond trees'. The town benefited from

*East Street north looking towards the harbour in the late nineteenth century*

the development of local industries, especially the sponge, pineapple and sisal industries during the late nineteenth century. The economy also benefited from improvements in telecommunications and the tourist industry in the early twentieth century.

# The twentieth century

The steady growth of the town was dramatically affected by Prohibition (1919–33) in the United States. Nassau's reputation as a trans-shipment centre for liquor which was bought by Americans and smuggled into the thirsty United States, caused a sudden upswing in the Bahamian economy. A flurry of building began. Great improvements were made in public utilities, including electricity and water supplies, and visitor accommodation and amenities were expanded. To cope with the increase in shipping, the harbour was dredged to a depth of 25 feet and Prince George Wharf was built. The Hotel Colonial, which was destroyed by fire in March 1922, was reconstructed and opened in February the next year. Slightly later, in 1926, Fort Montagu Hotel was built at Waterloo.

Along with the growth of tourism came the land boom. During the 1920s American investors began buying estates and cays, building homes and laying out modest developments on Hog Island and New Providence. Large estates and subdivisions, such as Westward Villas and the Grove Estate, were laid out. Land, changing hands at an unprecedented rate, increased enormously in value.

Air transportation linking Nassau with Miami began in 1929, the year of the Wall Street crash. Nassau suffered from the Depression that followed and also from the repeal of the Twenty-First Amendment which ended Prohibition. By the late 1930s, however, the economic climate had improved and Nassau was becoming recognized as a winter resort.

With the collapse of the sponging industry in 1938, and the outbreak of World War II during the next year, Nassau experienced dire economic problems. The city was saved by its strategic position in the Atlantic hemisphere. During the war it was chosen as a site of an Operational Training Unit under the joint auspices of the British and

United States Governments. The 'Project', that is the operation to expand Oakes Field and build Windsor Field, created thousands of war time jobs and was also the background against which a spontaneous labour riot occurred.

The post-war years witnessed a phenomenal growth in the tourist and banking industries which was reflected in the building of new hotels, and the expansion of Nassau to eastern, western and southern suburbs. By the beginning of the 1950s, Nassau was attracting not only the wealthy, titled and famous, but those in middle income brackets as well. Downtown Nassau could, in 1951, be called 'picturesque'. This was not the case for the Over-the-Hill district behind the city. In contrast to the architecturally attractive colonial town, which was dominated by the white elite, Over-the-Hill, where a large proportion of the population (mainly black) lived, was always much poorer and had more humble buildings. Its settlers lacked the necessary capital to develop it properly.

During the 1960s and 1970s, the growth of mass tourism and Nassau as a banking centre, stimulated changes in the city. The 1960s saw the beginning of the construction of large office blocks, and the further movement of city dwellers into the suburbs. By 1981 the city's boundaries had extended to include Mackey Street to the east, and Nassau Street to the west. Nassau, which was once a 'quiet sleepy hollow sort of place', had become a rapidly-expanding city, hectic, bustling and sometimes noisy. It has become a place of business whereas in the early days it was mainly residential. By the 1980s it contained vastly contrasting architectural styles, both old and new.

Downtown Nassau, unlike most cities in the Caribbean, has retained a distinct character, as Douglas Smith and Harold Munnings have demonstrated in *The Bahamian Architect*, 1995, 1996. Despite massive commercial and tourist developments since the 1950s, when most Caribbean colonies lost many old buildings, replacing them with modern architecture using plain, undecorated concrete and glass – downtown Nassau, despite losing many ancient edifices, replaced them not with (the soon to be rejected) international style, but one more acceptable, the Bahamian Colonial style.

Perhaps, as Smith and Munnings argue, the historic nature of Nassau was saved by the extreme conservatism of the Public Board of Works, which until the early 1960s was responsible for approving all designs for buildings. The members of the Board liked and promoted the 'Bahamian Colonial style', a mixture of English Georgian and Colonial architecture from the southern United States.

The Board 'shunned' the architecture of the Caribbean and also the 'Spanish' and South Florida style. They strictly enforced the rules in order to preserve the Bahamian Colonial character of New Providence, particularly within the historic city of Nassau. The Board's concern and regulations, according to Smith and Munnings, succeeded in preserving the architectural character of Nassau, especially during a period of expansion and development.

Buildings constructed in the Bahamian Colonial style between 1940 and 1960 include the *Government High School*, now the *College of The Bahamas*, the *Eastern Public Library*, Mackey Street, the *Grant's Town* or *Southern Public Library* and the *Crown Lands Office* (now the Department of Lands and Surveys), East Bay Street.

Occasionally, however, there were exceptions to the rules. According to Douglas Smith and Harold Munnings, the first break with the Bahamian Colonial style was the 1945 *Tradewinds Building* east of the Royal Bank of Canada on Bay Street. The developer, a member of the Board of Works, convinced the other members to approve the building, which was higher than the three-storey limit and had a flat roof. The

Board, however, did insist on a false gable facing Bay Street to provide an 'illusion of conformity to normal standards'.

The *Bernard Sunley Building*, built in the early 1960s, was the first large office building in Nassau. It had elements of the Colonial style (pitched roof and classical columns) but the scale was new for the time.

Once the Public Board of Works, later the Department of Physical Planning, became more flexible and relaxed the rules because of pressure from the developers, it was difficult to control the strict adherence to style. One result was the construction of the main *Post Office Building* on the site of the old Malcolm property on East Hill Street.

In the three decades since 1970, there has been tremendous growth in tourism and the financial sector in The Bahamas, and especially in Nassau. As well as the Building Code (1975), the supervision of the Department of Physical Planning (1969) and the Special Architectural Committee, there have been individuals and organizations which have made Bahamians aware of the need for historic preservation. Institutions like The Bahamas National Trust, The Bahamas Historical Society, The Department of Archives, the Ministry of Tourism and the Central Bank of The Bahamas have been working for years to encourage and promote historic preservation.

A list of historic places has been prepared by the Department of Archives and The

*The Department of Archives, Mackey Street*

Bahamas National Trust, which has also sponsored six videos on Historic Nassau, Historic Over-the-Hill, and Historic Out Islands. Various exhibitions have been held.

The Department of Archives mounted an exhibition 'A Selection of Historic Buildings in The Bahamas' as early as 1975. The Bahamas National Trust mounted an exhibition of Robert Douglas' Sketches of Historic Places Throughout The Bahamas.

The Bahamas Government has, with the assistance of the Bacardi Company, restored Vendue House and converted it into The Pompey Museum of Slavery and

Emancipation. Similarly, the Central Bank, assisted by the Department of Archives, the Ministry of Works and Antique Warehouse, has restored Balcony House and converted it into a period museum. Historic Villa Doyle on West Hill Street, built in the 1860s (northern part) and the 1920s (southern part) will be restored and converted to become the National Art Gallery. The Ministry of Tourism and the Nassau Tourism and Development Board have funded an architectural study of Historic Nassau. Mr Jackson Burnside is the architectural consultant.

In the Family Islands, the Kiwanis Club of San Salvador, with help from the Rotary Clubs of Nassau, Operation Raleigh and the Department of Archives, restored the old gaol in Cockburn Town, San Salvador and converted it into a museum.

The Department of Archives advised the Legal Department on the drafting of the Antiquities, Monuments and Museums Act which was passed in 1998 to make provision for the designation of historic places and the preservation of the same.

Several books have been written on the subject of historic preservation and buildings. For example Seighbert Russell wrote *Nassau's Historic Buildings*, The Bahamas National Trust, 1980. Gail Saunders and Donald Cartwright produced *Historic Nassau*, Macmillan, London, 1979. The Department of Archives prepared *A Selection of Historic Buildings of The Bahamas*, Nassau, 1975 and Robert Douglas wrote *Island Heritage*, 1992. A most popular book, *Reminiscing, Memories of Old Nassau* by Valerie Moseley Moss, edited by Ronald G. Lightbourn, was published in 1999.

## Conclusion

Historic preservation is very important. Physical monuments assist in telling the Bahamas' story and history. Many historic buildings have been demolished and destroyed. The face of Nassau has changed dramatically since the 1940s.

We cannot preserve all our historic buildings, but we can try to preserve those in zoned-off areas, for example those in the old city of Nassau, in Dunmore Town, Harbour Island and in New Plymouth, Green Turtle Cay, Abaco to name just a few. These historic buildings are a part of the Bahamian heritage. They tell of our past and form a part of our cultural identity. By preserving historic buildings Bahamians can, as they have in Charleston, South Carolina, capture 'a time in history and a way of life' when Nassau was a quiet little town and 'nice looking' with clean and shaded streets.

Although The Bahamas must move forward and welcome progress, new businesses and ideas, it must not fail to preserve the charm and history of the town of Nassau and other parts of The Bahamas. Without historic buildings, Nassau, like Charleston in South Carolina, would be like any other American city, with no feeling of historic or particular interest to its citizens or the millions of tourists who visit its shores annually. Heritage and eco-tourism are developing rapidly and The Bahamas, in order to keep pace as a leader in tourism, must look beyond sun, sea and sand which have attracted tourists for decades, to our material heritage. Bahamians can see examples of heritage preservation efforts in Barbados and Jamaica, including, for instance, changes of use for buildings, where historic private homes have been converted into restaurants, art galleries, museums, shops, etc. The Bahamas, like the Caribbean generally, 'is more than a beach' it is a country 'with its own integrity, history and culture'.

# *1* Public Square

The *Public Buildings*, which originally overlooked the harbour, were constructed between 1805–1816 on the north-eastern end of Parliament Street facing Bay Street. The three buildings initially housed the Post Office, Legislative Council, Court Room (centre building) Colonial Secretary's Office and Treasury (left) and the House of Assembly, Surveyor-General's Office and Provost Marshall's Office (right). They are of Loyalist influence being based on Governor Tryon's Palace in New Bern, the ancient capital of North Carolina.

*House of Assembly, Main Entrance.* The plaque on the right, commemorates the grant of these islands (formal annexation of The Bahamas) by His Majesty King Charles the First, to Sir Robert Heath, Attorney General of England, on 30th day of October 1629.

The *Statue of Sir Milo Butler,* located in Rawson Square, was sculptured by the late Randolph Johnston and erected in 1984. Sir Milo Butler was the first Bahamian Governor-General (1973–9) in an independent Bahamas. *Rawson Square* (above), the city's centre, was named after Governor Sir R. W. Rawson 1864–8.

The *Statue of Queen Victoria,* located in Parliament Square, was unveiled on 24 May, 1905 by Governor Sir William Grey Wilson (1904–12).

The *Supreme Court* Building, constructed between 1920–1, is situated south of the public buildings. It originally housed the Supreme Court, the Magistrates Court, the Registry, the Jury Room, the Chambers of the Chief Justice, the Attorney General and the Law Library.

The *Cenotaph*, a memorial to Bahamians who died in World Wars I and II, originally stood on the Frederick Street Steps. Constructed by W. V. Eneas in 1925, the Cenotaph was moved to its present site, between the Supreme Court and Nassau Public Library buildings, after World War II. The surrounding 'Garden of Remembrance' was developed during 1950.

# 2 Adjoining area

The *Royal Victoria Hotel,* was built by the Government between 1859–61 to accommodate winter visitors. It opened at the beginning of the American Civil War and very quickly became a popular rendezvous for Blockade Runners and officers of the Confederate army. After the Civil War business declined, but the Royal Victoria Hotel was revived in 1898 when H.M. Flagler purchased and renovated it. On 18 January, 1899, it was 'lighted with electricity' for the first time. After 1950 it changed hands several times, closing in 1971. It was re-purchased by the Government during the next year but perished by fire in 1991.

The *Nassau Public Library* was built between 1798–9 by Loyalist Joseph Eve to serve as a prison. At the first and second floors a central area opens onto vaulted spaces, which were originally prison cells, but now are used to house books and to serve as reading niches. A gallery surrounds the third floor from which a bell was rung to summon members of the House of Assembly to meetings. In 1873 this stone- constructed, octagonally-shaped building was converted into a Public Library, Reading Room and Museum. The building is said to have been inspired by the Old Powder Magazine in Williamsburg, Virginia.

*Curry House*, a three-storey building once annexed to the Royal Victoria Hotel on Shirley Street, was opened in 1890 as a private hotel owned by Mr R.H. Curry. Curry House was acquired by the Government in 1972 and is now used as offices.

The *Churchill Building,* which houses the Cabinet Office and the Public Treasury, was built in the early 1960s. It stands on the site of the old Adderley building.

# 3 Bay Street

Designed by Joseph Elias Dupuch, the *Masonic Building* on Bay Street is situated on the south side near Charlotte Street. The Masonic Temple's cornerstone was laid in July 1882 and the building was dedicated in 1885. The Masonic Grand Lodge 242 held meetings there.

Modern view of *Bay Street*, originally called 'The Strand', is almost certainly the oldest street in Nassau. It bounded the town on the north and originally ran along the sea. Now, much of the sea to the north of Bay Street has been reclaimed and business premises built. History was made on 31 May, 1998, when a $1.1 million traffic reversal plan for Nassau's downtown area came into effect. British driving regulations still exist, i.e. driving on the left.

The *British Colonial Hilton Hotel*, 1 Bay Street, is constructed on the sites of the former Fort Nassau (c.1695), the old military Barracks (c.1837) and the earlier Hotel Colonial erected between 1899/1900. Hotel Colonial, built by Henry Flagler, was destroyed by fire in March 1922. The Government re-purchased the property and signed a 10-year contract with The Bahamas Hotel Company (a subsidiary of the Munson Steamship Line). Begun in July 1922, the new Colonial Hotel was miraculously rebuilt and completed by February 1923. It was purchased by Sir Harry Oakes in 1939 and renamed the British Colonial Hotel. The hotel was later operated by the Sheraton Group and eventually sold by the Oakes Family. In 1977, RHK Capital of Toronto, Canada purchased, restored and renovated the property, maintaining its historic character. It re-opened on 4 December, 1999 as the British Colonial Hilton, a world-class luxury hotel complex and financial centre, in the heart of downtown Nassau.

*Statue of Woodes Rogers*, first Royal Governor of The Bahamas 1718–21; 1729–32 is displayed at the entrance of the British Colonial Hilton. In earlier days, *Blackbeard's Well*, said to have been used by Blackbeard 'to water his ships', was also known to be in the hotel grounds.

The *'Diocesan Building'* constructed in 1893, formerly housed St Cuthbert's, an Anglican church, known as the 'Seamen's Mission'. It was used by the Anglican Church to provide services for the sponge fishermen in the late nineteenth and early part of the twentieth century. It was later used as a Sunday School by Christ Church Cathedral and later still by June (Munnings) Stevenson as a photographic studio and Albertha Granger as a Fashion and Dress Design Centre. It now houses a T-Shirt outlet and a restaurant.

The *Pompey Museum of Slavery and Emancipation* at *Vendue House*. A building appears on a plan of Nassau as early as 1769 on the site on which Vendue House now sits. The 'new' Vendue House, a single storey arcaded building, constructed in the early 1800s, served as an auction market where everything, including slaves, was sold. During the early twentieth century (c.1913) the building was remodelled (a second storey was added) for the use of the Telegraph, Telephone and Electrical Departments. After The Bahamas Electricity Corporation relocated, the building was restored by the

Government between 1991 and 1992 with a grant from the Bacardi Company. It was converted into the Pompey Museum and officially opened in 1993. It is named after Pompey, a slave who led a revolt in defiance of the threat of being moved from one of Lord John Rolle's plantations on Exuma.

*Colombian Emeralds* occupies the former *City Pharmacy* Building which dates to the early 1850s. It has been traced to the 1854 purchase of Abraham Turton Holmes. Upon his death in 1908, the property was inherited by his two sons, Frank and Alfred, one of whom became Dr Frank Holmes, who attended to many Nassau families in the 1920s. The City Pharmacy remained in the Holmes family until 10 June, 1940 when it was sold to Siegfried Co. Ltd. In 1950 it was purchased by Kelly's Lumber Yard, owned by Trevor, Charles and Mary Ethel Kelly. Major renovations since 1997 (still going on early 2000) have restored this block of buildings beautifully. Holdings are in the name of Rovert Properties, owned by Mrs John (Betty) Kenning.

*The Island Shop* on Bay Street was built in the late twentieth century. It was owned by a colourful character and merchant, Howard Nelson Chipman in the 1920s through the 1940s. Mr Chipman's general store was called the London Shop which sold just about anything. The shop was later sold to Lofthouse Agencies, 1961–7, and then to British American Insurance Co., 1967–77. Since 1977 it has been owned by the Lee family and sells books, Kodak products, greeting cards and clothing.

The *Royal Bank of Canada*, established in 1869, opened its first branch in Nassau in 1908, with a staff of three, in a building some few doors from its present site on Bay Street. Sir George Henry Gamblin (born 28 June, 1870, died 2 October 1930), Member of the House of Assembly from 1901–24, President of the Legislative Council from 1924–30 and Member of the Executive Council 1908–30, was the Royal Bank's first manager. The Gamblin Memorial on Parliament Street was erected in his honour. Constructed in 1919, the Royal Bank building has seen many improvements internally, but it still maintains most of the original façade. Today its employees number nearly 600 and its branches spread throughout nine of the Bahama Islands.

*John Bull*, 284 Bay Street, is located on the site of the original Bahamas Ironmongery which preceded the Nassau Shop building erected 1955–7. The Nassau Shop opened in January, 1957, housing at the time 'the most modern, best equipped men's and women's shop in The Bahamas'. John Bull (established 1929), renovated and restored the building in 1996, with an official opening on 20 June, 1997. John Bull specializes in watches, jewellery, perfumes, leather goods, cameras and other luxury items.

*Fendi,* Bay and Charlotte Streets, is located in a nineteenth-century building which formerly housed G.R. Sweeting, a dry-goods store which relocated to Palmdale and is now closed. Fendi, owned by Joan and Chester Thompson, sells goods which include handbags, luggage, watches and fragrances.

*Solomon's Mines*, established in 1954, is located in a restored building (dating to the late nineteenth or early twentieth century) on Bay Street, between Parliament and Charlotte Streets. During renovation workmen found an old concrete ceiling beam dating to the early 1900s. On it was painted the name Solomon's Mines.

# *4* West Bay Street

*Sandals Royal Bahamian Hotel.* This picturesque hotel, located on Cable Beach, was formerly the Balmoral Beach Hotel. The latter developed out of the Balmoral Club which was built by Sir Oliver Simmonds in the early 1940s as an exclusive private members beach club for wealthy winter residents and visitors. Bahamians and non-members had to be invited. The original structure has been enlarged and renovated on a number of occasions and since 1997 houses the upmarket Sandals resort.

*Old Fort,* located on the western end of New Providence, was built near the remains of a late eighteenth century fort at the entrance of a small land-locked harbour called Lightbourne Creek. Old Fort is situated on a former plantation known as *Charlotville* and may include a part of the eighteenth century structure. The property has been owned by several leading Nassau families including the Malcolms, Adderleys and Menendez. Around 1912, Dr Charles S. Dolley, a physician and retired American professor, bought the estate (which grew sisal at that time), and added to the existing buildings. Old Fort was acquired in the 1920s by the grandfather of Nicholas F. Brady, US Secretary of the Treasury under Presidents Bush and Reagan. Later, Suydam Cutting, the well-known explorer, lived at 'Old Fort'. Unoccupied since 1964, the property was purchased in 1967 by the Old Fort Bay Co. Ltd (a subsidiary of The New Providence Development Co.) and serves as the cornerstone of the Old Fort Development.

# 5 Shirley Street

*Shirley Street* was named after Governor William Shirley (1758–68) who initiated a new survey of the town and reclaimed much swampy land, enabling the town to expand eastwards.

*Magna Carta Court*, constructed of cut stones and wood on the north-west corner of Parliament and Shirley Streets, dates to the 1780s. The property was once owned (1785–1802) by Robert Duncombe, a Loyalist, and David Rogers, a settler. Aaron Dixon, a Scot, who came to The Bahamas and established a business on Shirley Street, purchased Magna Carta Court in 1802. He died in 1809 and his will stipulated that the house should be rented and after maintenance was paid, the residue should be used to educate fatherless children.

After a special act was passed, the Vestry of Christ Church sold it in 1860 to Sarah Elizabeth Sears Alday, whose daughter Maria conveyed the property to her son, Walter K. Moore (later Sir Walter). He later sold it to Dawson Roberts who restored Magna Carta Court which now houses the firm of E. Dawson Roberts and Company. The building was once used as a bakery and an old oven has been preserved.

*James Knowles' Law Office* was built in the early twentieth century as a residence. The property was sold to Rodney McDonna in 1910. He sold it to William T. Saunders in March 1916. Mr Saunders probably built the house and lived there for many years. It was later owned by Dawson Roberts who restored it and sold it to Attorney-at-law, James Knowles, to house his Chambers. He still owned it in 1999.

*Addington House*, on Shirley Street and Sands Road leading into Elizabeth Avenue, was built in the 1860s. The former official residence of the Anglican Bishop of Nassau, The Bahamas and the Turks and Caicos, it was given to the Diocese in 1876 by Bishop Addington Venables, the second Bishop of the Diocese. It is said that Bishop Venables purchased the house from a former Chief Justice of the Colony and that it had once been occupied by the commandant in charge of Fort Fincastle. Today, Addington House is being restored.

*Zion Baptist Church* was built during the pastorship of the Revd Joseph Burton of the Baptist Missionary Society of Great Britain. It opened for public worship on 28 August 1835. The Church was destroyed by hurricane in 1929 and rebuilt under the leadership of the Revd Talmadge Sands. The church was expanded several times, especially under the Revd Charles Smith who succeeded the Revd Sands.

The *Princess Margaret Hospital*, formerly The Bahamas General Hospital, renamed in honour of Princess Margaret's visit in 1955, was originally founded in 1809. It is believed that the auxiliary building shown here was built about 1840.

Built on the site of several older buildings, The *Bahamas Financial Centre* was officially opened on 21 May, 1992 to house the Finance Corporation of The Bahamas. FINCO is 75 per cent owned by the Royal Bank of Canada and 25 per cent by the Bahamian public. Other world standard banking and off-shore financial services housed at the Financial Centre include Chase Manhattan, J.P. Morgan, Citco Bank & Trust, Dominion Bank, Credit Suisse, Bank Leu, UCF Trading, Equity Management, Banco Santander, Royal Bank of Scotland and others.

*The Tribune Building*, Shirley Street, was completed in 1963 and stands on the site of earlier structures. One of the two family cottages on this site was turned into offices, which subsequently housed *The Tribune*, a daily newspaper established 21 November, 1903 by Leon E.H. Dupuch, publisher/editor from 1903–14. His son Etienne (later Sir Etienne) served as publisher/editor 1919–72 and contributing editor 1972–91. Granddaughter Eileen Dupuch-Carron succeeded as publisher/editor from 1972 to the present. Mr and Mrs Roger Carron own *The Tribune*.

The *Collins House*, between Shirley Street and Collins Avenue, was built during the Prohibition years by Ralph G. Collins, a businessman, to replace a former residence badly damaged in the 1929 hurricane. After his death, the property was sold to St Andrews School which occupied the site between September 1950 and November 1971. The property was then purchased by the Government to house the Ministry of Education. The latter is being relocated and Collins House will be used for another purpose.

*The Bahamas Historical Society*, Elizabeth Avenue and Shirley Street, founded in 1959 by Lady Arthur, was built by The Imperial Order, Daughters of the Empire in the early twentieth century as its headquarters. It was donated to The Bahamas Historical Society in 1976. It now serves as the permanent headquarters of the Society and its Museum.

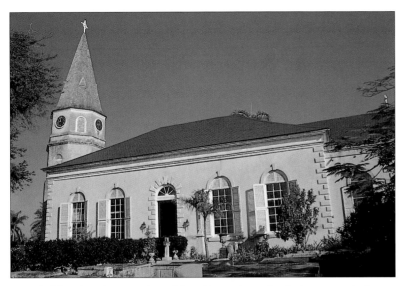

*St Matthews Anglican Church*, Shirley Street, was built between 1800 and 1802 by Joseph Eve, a Loyalist. The first Rector, the Revd Henry Groombridge, conducted the opening service on 18 July, 1802. The sermon was preached by Revd Robert Carter, the Rector of Christ Church. St Matthew's is the oldest extant church building on New Providence and most likely The Bahamas. Its architechture includes the early Roman style windows and octagonal tower with steeple – the latter added in 1816. The church was enlarged in 1887 and a stained-glass east window was placed in memory of Bishop Robert Peel Venables, who died on 8 October, 1876. Other renovations to improve the interior of the building have been made, however the original edifice of St Matthews remains unchanged. Father James Palacious, Rector for the past 11 years, was preceded by Canon Kirkley Sands.

The *Ebenezer Methodist Church*, Shirley Street, was built on the site of an earlier structure (c. 1802) by the Revd William Turton, first Methodist Missionary to come to The Bahamas in 1800. The foundation stone of the present Ebenezer Church was laid on 29 March, 1839 and the new church was opened for worship in 1841. Most of the new eighteenth century 'Meeting House' was destroyed in the 1929 hurricane. It was completely restored and improved then and over the years. Major renovations during 1957–62, under the ministry of the Revd Norman Pratt, altered and restored the floors, pews and pulpit, choir stalls and the central staircase. The Revd Charles Sweeting, Chairman of the Methodist Church of The Bahamas, has been a member of Ebenezer from 1957 to the present time.

# *6* East Bay Street

*Red Roofs* was built for Joseph and Jane C. Musgrove by John Dillett & Son around 1890. Constructed of timber, it features carved wooden jalousies, railings, posts and beautiful cupulas. The whole cellar, porch railings, fence and posts are built of solid mahogany. On Joseph Charles Musgrove's death in 1916, the house was auctioned to pay off his debts. It was bought by Charles Bethell and changed hands several times before it was purchased by Sir Roland T. Symonette, first Premier of The Bahamas. Since 1987 Red Roofs was operated as Roscoe's gourmet delicatessen and restaurant by the Darville family. Retained by the Symonette estate, it is now used as offices.

*The Temple*, c. 1879, is a two-storeyed residence constructed of the finest imported Jacksonville pine. It was built by Alphonso Brice for Kenneth and Eric Solomon (the late uncle and father respectively of Norman Solomon) as part of their family estate. The Temple has been the residence and studio of renowned Bahamian artist Brent Malone for 30 years. It is owned by the R.T. Symonette family and is now used as offices.

*601 Nightclub* is part of the former Symonette Shipyard founded on Hog Island in 1923 which moved to East Bay Street in 1938. Many wooden-hulled mail and freight boats were constructed there during the 1940s–50s and boat repairs continued until the late 1980s. The original three marine railways, using 'chains' to pull boats out of the water, gave way to modern technology of travel lifts. In the late 1980s a blacksmith's shop was added to the property which now houses a freight terminal and the 601 Nightclub. During their youth, the late Robert H. 'Bobby' Symonette, Sir Durward Knowles and Attorney Dawson E. Roberts had 'jobs' at the shipyard. The shipyard was established by the late Sir Roland T. Symonette (knighted in 1959 and became first Premier of The Bahamas in 1964) and is now owned by Lady Symonette.

*Sir Milo Butler's House*, located on Ernest Street, 'The Pond', is dated c. 1936. The two-storeyed traditional Bahamian house, built by Milo B. Butler, still stands. Since the 1930s, Sir Milo Butler agitated for the rights of the masses. He was elected to the House of Assembly in 1937 and after joining the PLP party in the 1950s, became a Minister following its 1967 victory. On 1 August, 1973, he was appointed the first Bahamian Governor-General in an independent Bahamas.

*Laurelhurst-By-The-Sea* (The Worrell House) c. 1935, was built on the site of an earlier structure erected in the early 1900s and owned by the late Jimmy Kelly. Dr G.S. and Mrs Mami Worrell purchased the home in 1919. The original house was destroyed by fire in 1934. A second storey for guests was added to the new structure in 1952. The Worrells accommodated black visitors to Nassau in the days when segregation was rife and they were not allowed in the major hotels.

*Toogood's Studio*, built around 1900, between East Bay and Williams Streets, was originally owned by John Pinder, a merchant. John Pinder married Sophia Moxey, whose niece Miss Thompson (married W.E. Pritchard, father of Sir Asa Pritchard) inherited the property in 1924. It was later acquired by Percival M. Lightbourn (father of Ronald G. Lightbourn), who passed 'Seaway' on to his daughter, Leone Lightbourn-

Wightman. It was purchased in the 1970s by Stanley Toogood, sold to Dr Cleary and purchased again by Stanley Toogood. His son Michael operates Toogood's Studio there. Stanley Toogood established his first photo studio on Bay Street in 1937, in the former Men's Shop building (now the site of John Bull).

The *Pink Pearl*, now an elegant restaurant, was built as a residence in the early twentieth century. It was owned by Orlando Pritchard in 1907 and later sold to Herbert A. McKinney, a member of the Executive Council. Mr McKinney leased the property to Alfred de Marigny, who married Nancy Oakes, daughter of Sir Harry Oakes. De Marigny operated a chicken farm in the gardens. He was charged but acquitted of Sir Harry Oakes' murder. Andrew McKinney also lived at Pink Pearl, which he named *Jumbay*, between c.1948 and 1968. The current owners, Jennifer and Christian Saunders, restored the house beautifully.

*Pink-un* dates to the 1920s and was originally a part of the Daniel and Edwin Moseley estate. Valeria Moseley Moss records that in the 1950s, John Steinbeck, the famous author of *Grapes of Wrath*, lived in the 'Pink-un' while writing one of his novels. Also, Sir Durward and Lady Knowles spent their early married life in this house. The 'Pink-un' is now owned by Neko and Patricia Meicholas. Moseley Lane, originally Western Cemetery Lane, was renamed in honour of George Moseley, who lost his life while serving in the Royal Air Force during World War II.

The 'original' *Hermitage*, constructed about 1790, was built by Lord Dunmore (Governor 1787–96) as a summer residence. It stood on property extending from the west boundary of 'Stanley' east to Dick's Point. The house has since been owned by a Mr Whylly, a Mr Dames, Mr Timothy Darling and in the 1880s by an English lady, a Miss Stuart. Between 1918–22 the house was 'added to' and was purchased in 1932 by Cardinal William O'Connell, Archbishop of Boston, who later bequeathed it to the Roman Catholic Diocese of Nassau. It has remained the official residence of the Roman Catholic Bishop of Nassau. *The Hermitage* is built of stone, cement and native hardwood.

The property known as *Sunnyside* was acquired in 1838 by W. J. Weech, a prominent Bay Street merchant. The original country home on this site had a splendid view of the harbour. Upon Mr Weech's death, the property was inherited by his daughter, Mary Lockhart-Weech, who married the Revd Francis Moon, an English Methodist Minister in The Bahamas. The property was inherited by their daughter, Mary Beatrice Moon Lightbourn, who bequeathed Sunnyside to her daughter Winifred (who married Mr Mervyn Johnson in 1939). Three generations of Moons have honeymooned at Sunnyside.

# 7 East Hill Street

*Jacaranda*, formerly 'Anderson House', located on East Hill and Parliament Streets, was built by Sir George Campbell Anderson in c.1840s using ballast stones from Georgia. Although remodelled, it retains much of its original structure i.e. alternating chamfered quoins, wide latticed verandahs and traditional jalousies. Nancy, Baroness von Hoyningen-Huene (née Oakes), inherited Jacaranda from her sister Mrs Shirley Oakes Butler whose mother purchased it in 1949. (See page 7 for more information.)

*Jacaranda* (rear view)

*East Hill* (Ministry of Foreign Affairs) was originally built of cut limestone in the early 1800s. It was the former home of the prominent Matthews family. Briefly owned by Lords Beaverbrook and Kensley, it was next acquired by the late American businessman, S.K. Wellman of Cleveland, who converted it into the exclusive East Hill Club in the early 1960s. It was purchased in the 1980s by Carlton Williams, who restored and renovated it. The photograph includes the original kitchen with rainwater tank dated 1843. The Ministry of Foreign Affairs has been housed there since 1987. (See page 6 for more information.)

*Hillcrest* or *Bank House*, at St Andrew's Court, was constructed in the mid-nineteenth century. Edwin Charles Moseley, founder of *The Nassau Guardian* (1844), owned and occupied it. For many years *The Nassau Guardian* was produced there. Hillcrest was later sold to Mr Glen Stewart and is now owned by Trasco Holdings Ltd. (See page 6, for more information.)

# $8$ Government House

*Government House*, situated on a site known as Mount Fitzwilliam (named after a former Governor of the colony who lived there around 1737), was built originally between 1803 and 1806. The eastern wing was demolished and replaced between 1929 and 1932. The house has been restored and redecorated several times. (See page 7 for more information.)

This statue of *Christopher Columbus*, situated on the steps of Government House, was modelled in London by Washington Irving. Governor Sir James Carmichael Smyth (1829–33) imported and presented it to the 'Colony of The Bahamas' in 1830. Christopher Columbus' three-ship fleet, the *Santa Maria*, *Nina* and *Pinta*, brought him to The Bahamas in his attempt to 'discover' a route to Asia. On 12 October, 1492, Columbus landed on Guanahani, which he renamed San Salvador.

# *9* West Hill Street

The original building on the site of *Graycliff* is believed to have been erected in the 1720s. Most of the present structure probably dates to the mid-nineteenth century. The house is built of stone and wood in the traditional Bahamian vernacular architectural style. (See pages 7–8 for more details.)

*West Hill House* (10 West Hill St). This wooden building dates to the early-mid nineteenth century and is situated immediately west of Graycliff. It was once occupied by Edward St George, Chairman of the Grand Bahama Port Authority and at one time was owned by Sir Robert McAlpine. Enrico Garzaroli, the present owner of Graycliff, purchased West Hill House in 1995 and made it his home.

*Villa Doyle* was constructed in the mid-1860s. The original northern section was built by William Henry Doyle, Chief Justice of The Bahamas and Sir Walter K. Moore added on the southern two-storey section in the 1920s. The mansion is being restored to house the National Art Gallery of The Bahamas. (See page 8 for more details.)

*Postern Gate* and its complex of buildings on the southern side of West Hill Street is believed to have been built in the 1840s. It has been renovated several times and now houses the Graycliff Cigar Company and the Humidor Restaurant. (See page 8 for more details.)

The original structure of *Ranora House* dates to the late 1860s. Known as St Mary's Villa, it once served as the rectory for St Mary the Virgin Anglican Church on Virginia Street. The house was bought in 1939 by Cora Munson of the Munson Steamship Lines and renamed Ranora House. The entrance was changed from West Hill to the eastern courtyard and the east and west wings were added c.1930– 40s. Ranora House served as a temporary home for the Governor of The Bahamas, Sir Ralph Grey (1964– 8) and is now owned by Eric and Betty Cottell, who are keen to preserve West Hill Street. (See page 9 for more details.)

Window details of *Ranora House*.

The former *Sisters of Charity Convent* lies immediately east of Ranora House and was built in the late 1880s to accommodate the Sisters of Charity of The Roman Catholic church. It has since been gutted and there are plans to restore it. (See pages 9–10 for more details.)

The *O'Donnell House* is believed to have been built in the early nineteenth century. It has been restored and renovated and is renowned for the famous people, such as Lord Mountbatten and HRH Prince Charles, who have stayed at or visited the house. (See page 10 for more details.)

*The Fold* was constructed around 1840. An 1864 print shows the 'core' of this building with quoined corners. The western and eastern sides were probably added later.

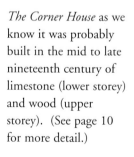

*The Corner House* as we know it was probably built in the mid to late nineteenth century of limestone (lower storey) and wood (upper storey). (See page 10 for more detail.)

# *10* East Street

*East Street* – the eastern boundary of the early town of Nassau.

*Cascadilla,* East Street and Millar's Court, was built in the 1840s. At one time a plantation house occupied the property with outside kitchens and slave cottages. It was the home of Dr William Kirkwood MD, an Irishman, who arrived in the Colony and practised medicine there for nearly fifty years. The house was sold to Edward George, son of the founder of John S. George, and later to John Tinker and the late Sir Harold Christie who lived there. Later it was converted into the H.G. Christie Real Estate office. Sold again, the building is now in a ruinous condition and its present owner has been asked to restore it.

Built of cut stone walls, the *H.G. Christie Ltd.* building dates to the late nineteenth century. It was the residence of Christopher Esfakis (father of Dr Andrew Esfakis) from the 1920s–50s who operated a sponge business at this property. Since the 1960s it changed hands to Lord Dudley, the late Sir Harold G. Christie (founder of the company) and to Sir Thomas M. McAlpine. It was purchased in 1996 by William McP 'Peter' Christie who renovated the entire building. HGC is the oldest real estate company in The Bahamas and recently celebrated 75 years of business.

*Media House* was probably built in the late nineteenth century. It has been owned by several persons, the most recent being Wendall K. Jones, operator of radio station Love '97 and the daily newspaper, *The Bahama Journal*.

The building in which *Best Ever (Mortimer's) Candy Kitchen* is located was owned by William B. North, merchant, who sold to Mr Ulric J. Mortimer in the 1940s. It was constructed in the early 1900s and has been renovated several times. Ulric J. Mortimer Sr, born in Inagua in 1908, was a pioneer in the local candy manufacturing business. He established the Best Ever Candy Company in 1935 in his home on Hospital Lane and later moved it to East Street. where it prospered. Since Mr Mortimer's death in 1980, family members have operated it. It is currently undergoing renovations.

The *Police Headquarters*, once known as the *Police Barracks*, was erected in 1900 on the site of the old Agricultural Gardens on East Street. Much of the material from the old Military Barracks (located on the former site of Fort Nassau that was demolished at the end of the nineteenth century to make way for the construction of the Colonial Hotel) was used in the construction of the Police Barracks.

The *Old Prison* was built in the Police Barracks Compound in 1865. The Prison was later moved to the south of Sandilands Village (Fox Hill). The old Prison served as the Parcel Post for some years and has now been converted into offices for the Royal Police Force Officers.

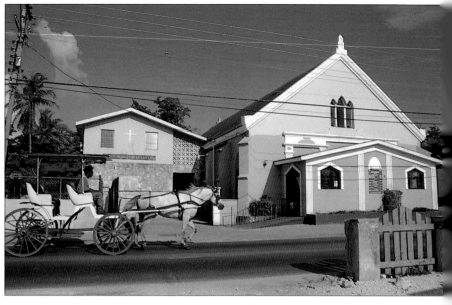

The *Church of God*, built between East Street and Lily-of-the Valley corner in 1952, had its headquarters in Cleveland, Tennessee. By 1910 its teachings extended to southern Florida where many Bahamians had migrated. Bahamians Edmond Barr and his wife, Rebecca, were among the converts. Returning to Nassau, they became missionaries of the Church of God. Assisted by R.M. Evans, a white American missionary, they successfully converted Arabella Eneas, who in turn, converted her husband William V. Eneas. The latter became the first Bishop of the Church of God in The Bahamas. Early meetings were held in homes and humble wooden structures but by the 1920s a more substantial building was erected at 'Eneas Jumper Corner'. The present Church of God Cathedral on East Street commenced in 1952 with Bishop W.V. Eneas as its pastor.

The *Church of God of Prophecy*. In 1922 a serious schism occurred in the mother Church of God in Tennessee and the Bahamian Church was forced to take sides. A few years later, a group left the Church of God (which was then led by W.V. Eneas) and set up their own Church, eventually building on Taylor Street. The Church of God of Prophecy, as it is now known, built its present tabernacle on East Street between 1945–6.

# 11 Parliament Street

*Parliament Street*, constructed between 1788 and 1813 was named after the Parliamentary buildings, the House of Assembly and Legislative Council (now the Senate Building), which stand at the foot of Parliament Street.

*Magistrate's Court 13,* located on Parliament Street, was originally erected as a chapel for the Salem Baptist congregation, on a site known as the 'Old Livery Stables grounds'. The wife of Baptist Minister, the Reverend Daniel Wilshere, laid the foundation stone on 24 May, 1893. The chapel was opened for public worship on 5 February, 1894. Salem Union Baptist Church built a new and more spacious church on Taylor Street and relocated. The original building is now used as a Magistrate's Court.

Believed to have been built by shipwrights in the 1860s, *Green Shutters* can be traced back to Bruce Lockhart Burnside who conveyed the property to the Hon. John Pinder on 27 March, 1865. It was passed to his daughter Virginia Ann (Mrs Frank Berry) in the 1920s. In 1947 Mrs Berry sold it to M. Ogilvy-Spence and in 1962 'Green Shutters' was purchased by Mr and Mrs Charles Bennett Warry. It became the popular *Ben Warry's* pub and restaurant during the 1960s-70s. It was purchased by Shirley Oakes Butler in the 1970s and leased out to operators of 'Green Shutters'. In 1999 two ambitious entrepreneurs, Michael Fowler and Sophie Wong, revived the 140 year-old restaurant property.

# *12* Charlotte Street

*Charlotte Street,* which appeared on the 1788 plan of Nassau, was named after George III's wife, Charlotte Sophia Frederick. The Charlotte Street Steps which connect the Charlotte and East Hill Streets were erected in 1864 and underwent repairs when Charlotte Street was being levelled and paved in 1915.

The *Malone ('Lace') House*, with its decorative lattice and fret work, was constructed in the mid–to late nineteenth century. It was acquired by the Revd Francis Moon, a Methodist Minister, in 1884. In 1936 Wilhelmina Malone purchased it from Adelaide Kemp, thus the name 'The Malone House'. It was owned by the Malones until 1974 when it was purchased by George Constantakis and is now used as a guest house.

The 1788 plan of Nassau shows a building on the site on which the *Cellar Restaurant* now stands. The old kitchen, with a large fireplace and oven to the east of the house, may date to 1788. However, the present structure was added later, perhaps in the 1840s. The Revd Francis Moon, Methodist Minister, spent some years in this residence. It was converted into a restaurant in the late 1970s. The wooden shutters, latticed verandah, wooden louvres and exterior wooden stairs are still part of its old world charm. The Cellar is owned by Claudette Nihon.

*Coin of The Realm* was built on the site of an earlier structure. The present edifice dates to the 1840s. Legend has it that this building was once used to store ammunition for Fort Nassau (now the British Colonial Hilton) to which it was supposedly linked by an underground tunnel. In recent years, it has been restored and renovated into a first class jewellery shop by the Brown and Stewart families.

*Victoria Hall,* named in honour of Queen Victoria, was built between 1887 and 1890 to house Queen's College, a Methodist high school which opened in 1890 and also operated a preparatory division. The precursor to Queen's College was the *Nassau Wesleyan Collegiate School.* Queen's College was later expanded and remained on the original site between Charlotte and Frederick Streets until 1961 when it relocated to Village Road.

The original section of *Aurora Lodge Hall* possibly dates to the 1860s. Friendly Societies and Lodges existed in the mid-nineteenth century, mainly for funeral and sickness benefits. Lodges became more popular in the late nineteenth and twentieth centuries. Many Lodges had affiliations with those in the United States.

# 13 Frederick Street, Princes and Duke Streets

*Frederick Street* appeared on the 1739 plan of Nassau and was presumably named after King George II's wife, Wilhelmina Caroline Frederick. Princes Street was named after their son, Frederick, Prince of Wales and Duke Street after George III's second son, Frederick, Duke of York and Albany.

*Frederick Street Steps* were constructed in the late nineteenth or early twentieth century to replace the road which ran from Frederick Street to East Hill Street. Frederick Street was cut out of rock and constructed in 1793. The original Cenotaph was built on the Frederick Street Steps in 1925.

Michael Malcolm, a Loyalist, was instrumental in getting *The Kirk* built. The cornerstone of *St Andrew's Presbyterian Church* was laid in August 1810. Since its inception, the Kirk has been renovated and restored, undergoing many architectural changes. The 'Sessions Room' was built in 1842. the belfry in 1844 and the spire in 1847. Later, in 1864, the northern transept (now the nave), portico and bell tower were added. The church was extensively renovated in the mid-twentieth century. It was re-roofed, the interior redecorated and redesigned and the Kirk Hall enlarged.

The foundation of *Trinity Methodist Church* was laid on 21 August, 1861 but due to various difficulties, it was not opened for worship until 2 April, 1865. On 1 October, 1866, the church was completely destroyed by a hurricane. Trinity Methodist Church was restored by Fred Dillet between 1868 and 1869.

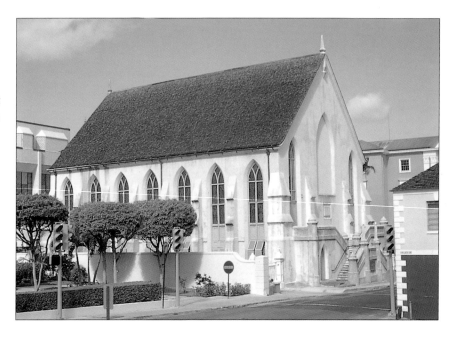

*Malcolm (Marmaduke) House* was built on a site owned by a Mrs Bell whose daughter married Marmaduke Sands in 1792. Built in two main stages, the eastern section, constructed mainly of wood, dated to about 1840. The western section built of stone was added around 1920. It was owned for a long time by the Malcolm family (hence the present name) and then sold to a private bank. While under renovation it was destroyed by Hurrricane Floyd in 1999. The property is now owned by The Central Bank of The Bahamas.

The *Rees building*, Frederick Street, dates to the mid-nineteenth century and was once owned by the Methodist Church. It served as the home of Methodist ministers and the headmasters of Queen's College before the building to the east was built to house them. In the late 1950s it was purchased by Dora Agnes Johnson whose husband Dr Hugh Johnson, established a dentist's office there. The property is now used for offices and is held in trust for grandson Colin T. Rees, son of Mrs Colin L. (Helen) Rees.

*Old Damianos House* 'Apsley House', 73 Frederick Street (situated in the Charlotte House complex built in the 1970s) is a three-storey building dating to the 1840s which once housed the officers of the West India Regiment. It is also said that 'Apsley House' once served as a Governor's Residence. It was acquired by the late Mr George Damianos around 1914 and sold to Robertson Symonette Ltd in the 1940s. It now houses the United European Bank & Trust, a subsidiary of UEB, Geneva, Switzerland.

Also contained in the Charlotte House complex is the façade of the last *Apsley House stables* for horses once used by the West India Regiment. The floor was of brick brought to Nassau as ballast by visiting sailing ships and the rafters were built with timbers salvaged from shipwrecks.

# *14* Market Street

*Market Street* was originally called Prison Lane, after the early prison located on this street. The prison was moved between 1799–1800 to the site which now houses the Nassau Public Library. The Market (built 1800–1) after which Prison Lane was renamed, was located on Bay Street at the northern end of Market Street.

*Gregory Arch* was built in 1852 by J.J. Burnside, Surveyor-General, who had laid out Grant's Town in the 1820s. The arch, which led from Market Street into 'Over-The-Hill' or Grant's Town, was named after Governor John Gregory (1849–53). The road over the arch led from East Hill Street into Government House.

The cornerstone of the *Central Bank* was laid in July 1973 by HRH Prince Charles who represented the Queen during the Independence ceremonies. Her Majesty, Queen Elizabeth II, officially opened the Central Bank on 20 February, 1975, during an official visit to The Bahamas with the Duke of Edinburgh. The Central Bank, successor to the Monetary Authority, was established in 1974. This 'birds-eye' view shows the Central Bank facing Market Street, surrounded by the 'Kirk' to the north, Trinity Methodist on the south-east corner and Balcony and Verandah houses in the foreground. The latter are under the Central Bank's preservation commitments.

*Balcony House*, a two-storey residence on Market Street, built around 1790 or even before, was constructed of American soft cedar. It is distinguished by its front upper balcony, which is partly supported by wooden knee brackets. Balcony House has an ancient detached kitchen and a mahogany staircase, said to have come from a ship. It was once owned by Charlotte Dillet and Lord Beaverbrook. Mrs John C. (Marie Josephine) Bryce (heir to the A&P Foodstore chain) acquired Balcony House in 1947. It was purchased by the Central Bank on 8 August, 1985. The Bank, assisted by the Ministry of Works and Utilities, Department of Archives and Antique Warehouse, restored the house in 1992–3 and converted it into the Balcony House Museum.

*Verandah House,* which is just north of Balcony House, was built of wood in about the 1790s. It has a stone cellar, dormer windows and a small porch with wooden rails. It is being restored by the Central Bank of The Bahamas.

*St Agnes Rectory*, Market Street. This traditional Bahamian house with its wrap-around verandahs, was built in 1925 to house the Rector of St Agnes' Anglican Church. Inducted in May, 1925, Father Herbert George was the first priest to marry in that parish. His bride was Dorothea Coleman. The late Archdeacon, William Thompson and his wife Rose, lived there for 32 years.

The *Butler Residence*, Market Street, is a well-kept, typical clapboard structure with decorative railings on the front and side porches, built in the early 1900s by contractor Gerald Rahming for Charles Turner Butler. Mrs Lois Butler-Wilson, his daughter (age 86), and granddaughter Yvonne Wilson, still live there. Melanie Roach, Director of Works, and Teresa Butler, a Permanent Secretary, are grandchildren of Charles T. Butler and his wife Ella Jane Evans-Butler.

The *Thompson Residence* (and Shop) is another typical example of a clapboard house built in the late 1920s or early 1930s by Mr and Mrs William Thompson Sr. The shop was probably added later. The late Archdeacon William Thompson, former Rector of St Agnes Church (1967–99), Suffragan Bishop Gilbert Thompson, former Rector of St Barnabas and surgeon, Dr Philip Thompson, grew up in this house.

# *15* George Street

*George Street* appeared on the 1739 plan of Nassau and was named after King George II (1727–60). It was earlier known as 'Maiden Street'.

*Lightbourn Building*, on the corner of George and Bay Streets, was constructed after the June 1942 fire. The original building on this site housed R.M. Lightbourn's Drug Store and Lightbourn's Studio (destroyed). The new building served as Lightbourn's Perfume Shop (established 1889) for many years. It now accommodates a store for men's clothes.

Just south of Christ Church Cathedral lies *C.A. Christie Real Estate* (formerly Lex House). This historic house with cellar, built around 1776, may be one of the oldest in Nassau. It possibly housed the Commander of the Spanish Garrison which occupied Nassau between 1782 and 1783. In the early 1900s it was owned and occupied by Dr and Mrs H. Mather Hare and family, then sold to Mr F.C. VanZeylan in the 1940s. It was purchased and restored by Roy Henderson in the late 1970s serving as a residence and law office. It was subsequently bought by C.A. Christie Real Estate who re-restored it beautifully.

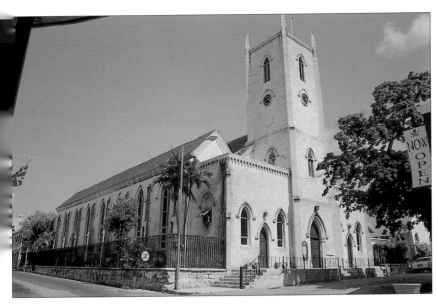

The present *Christ Church Cathedral* sits on the site of four former smaller churches. Its foundation stone was laid in 1837 and it opened for public worship in 1840, being consecrated in 1845 by Bishop Spencer of Jamaica, The Bahamas and Honduras. It was enlarged between 1864 and 1865. In 1861 Christ Church was constituted the Cathedral Church of the Diocese thus making the town, 'the City of Nassau.' The Cathedral was renovated in the mid-1990s.

*Christ Church interior.* The stone structure of Christ Church comprises a chancel, nave and two side aisles, and a western tower. The main entrance is through a central square clock tower from where a large *stained glass window* (original c.1868) comes to view over the altar. The damaged central window was replaced in 1945 and stained glass side windows were added in the 1990s. The timber trusses and arched braces are reminiscent of the original gothic style.

A building, presumably *Georgeside*, is indicated on the 1788 plan of Nassau. Georgeside originally consisted of two storeys and by 1830 the roof was raised some 10 feet to accommodate a third storey. The house is of white stucco with green shutters and doors. Beams located in the older part of the house were handhewn by ships' carpenters. There is an enclosed second storey verandah and an open one on the lower floor. A gingerbread railing spans the width of the house and porches. The original kitchen occupied a separate building at the back of the house with a large fireplace and oven. The fireplace and chimney still remain. The current owners are Ed and Lee Woodruff.

*Bostwick and Bostwick Chambers*, with lattice decoration, and formerly part of Dean's cottage, is another historic house, built around the 1880s. It was purchased by Henry and Janet Bostwick who renovated it for use as law chambers. The adjoining old kitchen, complete with original fireplace, oven, clay tiles and timbered beams, has been preserved.

On the corner of George and Duke Streets, another historic building complex remains. *Princess House*, also known as the *Glenton-Newton House*, is an important example of the Georgian architectural style imported to Nassau by the Loyalists. Built of limestone block and braced wooden construction, between 1788 and the early 1800s, the three-storey house consists of a simple rectangular plan. At the back is a two-storey block and wood building with bricks enclosing a limestone hearth. This building was used as a kitchen for the main house, as was common during and after the Loyalist period. This property, owned by Henry and Janet Bostwick, is scheduled for restoration.

Kitchen chimney of Princess House, c. late eighteenth century.

# *16* Marlborough Street

The *Pirates of Nassau Museum* formerly consisted of the Marlborough Arms, the 'Big Store' and the Lofthouse Property. The *Marlborough Arms*, with three gable windows, was built around the mid-nineteenth century. It was owned by Captain John Henry Bethel, father of the late Charles P. Bethel, a former Colonial Secretary who died in 1978. For many years the Bethels operated a bakery on this site, where remains of an old kitchen are still evident. The 'Big Store'

(really four stores in one, originally one storey, east of Bethel's bakery), owned by Wilfred Parliament (W.P.) Adderley, sold candy, fruit, dry goods, notions, shoes, hats and groceries. These properties, including Lofthouse, once owned by the powerful Lofthouse family, were renovated and restored to house the Pirates of Nassau, an interactive museum which highlights the pirate era in Bahamian history. The Museum opened in 1998.

*The Marlborough Arms*

# *17* Cumberland Street

This street is believed to have been named after one of George III's sons, Ernest, Duke of Cumberland.

A 1770 survey cites the property on which *Cumberland House* sits as the property of Phillip Brown. According to the *Bahamas Architect*, Summer 1995, the original two-storey building which faces Cumberland and Duke Streets, was built in 1775 'of quarried limestone block, mahogany, cedar shingle and native pine for the upper storey floor, porches and roof'. Cumberland House was beautifully restored in the 1990s. Anthony Jervis, preservationist architect, designed and oversaw this fine restoration project.

*Cumberland House*
inside the *Courtyard*.

*The Deanery* was built between 1802 and 1803 by the Vestry of Christ Church as a Parsonage House. It is a three-storeyed building of stone with chamfered quoins. It originally had verandahs on the east, west and north sides of the house. The original outside kitchen still stands. There is also a one-storey building with a fireplace and another area probably used as a sleeping area. This outhouse is believed to have been the slave quarters. The house has been altered over the years, but still contains many of its ancient features. It is still owned by Christ Church Cathedral.

*Hillside Manor* dates to c. 1847. It served as a Chief Justice's private residence. A kitchen at the rear of the building still stands. It contains the original fireplace with authentic bricks. The property was acquired by William 'Bill' Saunders in 1980 who restored the house and kitchen. The building now accommodates the offices of Majestic Tours.

# *18* Nassau Court

*Nassau Court* was named after Fort Nassau and the town of Nassau in honour of Prince Orange-Nassau, who became William III of England (1689–1702).

The building which houses the *Ministry of Environmental Health* (in 1999), sits at the southern end of Nassau Court, on the site of the West Chapel of the Wesleyan Methodist Church built in 1830. In 1864 the Town Chapel was purchased by the Bahamian Government to house the Boys Central School, which functioned until 1924. The Government High School (GHS), established in 1925, occupied the building from that date to 1960, when it moved to the new building on John F. Kennedy Drive, now occupied by the College of The Bahamas. After the building was vacated by GHS, it was occupied by the Ministries of Works, Tourism, Economic Affairs and then the Department of Environmental Health.

Window details (open and closed shutters) of the Environmental Health Building, Nassau Court (c.1830).

# *19* Queen Street

This street is thought to have been named after George III's wife Charlotte Sophia, who was crowned with him in 1761.

*Marlborough Antiques*, on the corner of Queen and Marlborough Streets, was constructed in the 1920s by a Mr Scarlatos (Greek) who made it his family home. The house was later converted into an upmarket dress shop named 'Francise', by Mrs Frank Christie (American).
At present it is the home of Marlborough Antiques operated by artist R. Brent Malone and June Knight.

*Devonshire House*, at 11 Queen Street, was built in about 1840. It is an outstanding example of Bahamian Colonial architecture. Its columned doorway, fretworked balconies, spacious rooms, deeply recessed windows and curved stairway are marks of gracious living in the mid-nineteenth century. The house was once owned and occupied by Joseph Elias Dupuch and his wife, Elizabeth Augusta. Mr Dupuch designed and oversaw the building of the Kirk Hall on Prince's Street, the Masonic Temple, Bay Street and other buildings in Nassau. The house was also once owned by an Archbishop of New York, M. A. Corrigan, Samuel J. Higgs and Eunice, Lady Oakes. It was restored by John Stuart in 1995–6 and sold to Lennox Paton and Company in 1996.

*28 Queen Street.* This three-storey house built of stone and wood was constructed in the 'old Colonial style' with louvres, lattice work dormers and the traditional porches. It was built in about 1830 and was once owned by Mr Charles Rutledge Burnside, son of J.J. Burnside, Surveyor-General of the Colony. The latter Burnside laid out Grant's Town in the 1820s and also built Gregory Arch which was opened in 1852. Charles R. Burnside sold the property to W.E. Pritchard, father of Sir Asa Pritchard. The Pritchard family lived in the house for some years and sold it to Mr John Brown, son of Sir Joseph Brown. It is now the property of Nancy (Oakes) Baroness Von Hoyningen Huene.

*30 Queen Street,* also recently named Garrison House, is constructed of cut squared stone and clapboard timber in the Bahamian Colonial style. It is believed to have been built between 1815 and 1825. A verandah shades the north-east, east and south sides of the building. Mr Ted Curry, former owner, purchased this historic building from Mr A.E. Creighton of Boston, Massachusetts who later sold it to interior decorator, Melville Doty. After occupying it for eight years, he sold it to its current owner, retired British banker, David Nicoll in 2001.

*Small Cottage,* 44 Queen Street, dates to about 1804. Records indicate that this cottage may be nearly 200 years old. It has an old fireplace with an original hardwood beam, chimney and a beautiful garden. It was once owned by Mr Ted Curry and Baron and Baroness Lysart and Irene Von Hoyningen Huene. It is now owned by Dr Sy Pierre and his wife Catherine Ramsingh-Pierre.

# *20* West Street

*West Street* was the western boundary of the early town of Nassau.

*International House* (Greenstreets), between West and Virginia Streets, is an historic building dating to the early 1800s. It has timber galleries, bracketed posts and unusual hipped dormers on its roof – probably reconstructed. International House was once the property of the late Mr Wilton Albury, who was the inspector of schools in The Bahamas, and purchased by Robertson, Ward and Associates in the 1950s who restored and renovated the then existing structure in 1959. This work was done in two stages and completed in 1961. During the first stage the kitchen,

which occupied a separate building to the south, was extended and converted to offices for the owners. The second stage involved modifications to the main structure. The architect, Mr Taylor Gates, tried to maintain the character of this stately residence. An unusual feature of this building is the large ten-foot deep cellar. The property has been obtained by International Business Centre, owned by Kendal Munnings.

*Yamacraw House*, 14 West Street, constructed of stone and timbers, is believed to have been built in the early twentieth century. This house is now owned by Anthony Jervis, a leading preservationist architect.

The *Annunciation Greek Orthodox Church* on West Street was built in 1932 to accommodate the Greek community. A number of Greek families migrated to The Bahamas at the end of the nineteenth and beginning of the twentieth century to engage in the sponge industry. In the early years, religious services were conducted on the premises of N.J. Mangos on Virginia Street. The Greek Church's congregation of twelve families in the early days has grown to well over 70 families at the present time.

The foundation stone of *St Francis Roman Catholic Church* was laid in August 1885, by Lady Georgiana Ayde-Curran, wife of Surgeon-Major, F.G. Ayde-Curran. The first public service was held there in early November, 1886 and in February, 1887 it was consecrated by the Archbishop of New York, Michael A. Corrigan. St Francis Xavier Cathedral, the first Roman Catholic church built in The Bahamas, has been renovated and enlarged several times.

# *21* Virginia Street

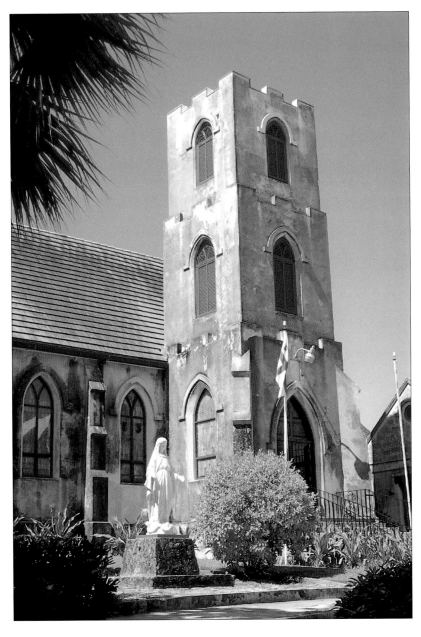

The site on which *St Mary's Church* was constructed was previously occupied by the 'Bray's School House'. St Mary's, used as a Chapel-of-Ease to Christ Church, was located in an older building which was destroyed in the hurricane of 1 October, 1866. The present church's foundation stone was laid in October 1868 and it was completed in April of the following year. Several additions and renovations have been made, including the bell tower, during the ministry of Canon Edward G. Holmes. The current Rector is Canon Warren H. Rolle who was preceded by Father Peter Grist (1979–97).

*Dagbros*, Virginia Street, occupies two buildings parts of which may date to
the mid-nineteenth century. A conveyance from Hester Stout to William
Armbrister dated 28 August, 1863, records that there were houses, outhouses,
gardens and fences on the site. The timber house was recorded to Mr D.J.
DeGregory from 1938–60s. The stone house, with a cellar and outside
kitchen built of cut stone, was purchased in 1938 by Mr Cecil Edward M.
Jones, an electrician. His father Erskine Jones, served as Imperial lighthouse
keeper. The house became the Cecil Jones Electric building and homestead in
which nine brothers and three sisters grew up. It is presently used as offices
and owned by businessman Vincent D'Aguilar.

*Christofilis Villa*, home of the
Christofilis family, was built around
1900. Constantine and Adrienne
Christofilis came to Nassau in 1898
on their honeymoon and to engage
in the sponge business. (They were
the second Greek family to settle in
The Bahamas, George and Aristede
Damianos came before them).
They purchased the property in
1900 and established a sponge shed
which, during the profitable years,

employed 22 women to clip and trim sponges and eight men to work the presses and bales. Winifred Christofilis (wife
of the late Jack Christofilis) still occupies the house. The sponge shed also still exists and is presently in use.

# 22 Delancey Street

*Buena Vista*, in Delancey Street, is believed to have been built in 1790. The land on which it stands was owned by Lord Dunmore and later by the Anglican Church. While Lord Dunmore owned the estate, Delancey Street and Delancey Town had not been developed. In 1846–7, the house was occupied by an English Colonial official, probably Stephen Delancey, after whom the street and Delancey Town were named. It was later occupied as a private residence by Mr and Mrs Edward S. Toothe who converted it into a restaurant and guest house. Buena Vista has changed hands several times and remains a fine restaurant operated by Mr and Mrs Stan Bocus. It was believed a tunnel once joined the cellar of Buena Vista to Fort Charlotte.

*International Travellers Lodge ('Sidney House' – Eldon Homestead)* Delancey Street. This 'clapboard', wood constructed house, was built in 1926 by the Hon. Sidney Eldon, who served as Assistant Treasurer and Comptroller of Customs. He married Rowena Hill. Their two children, the Rt Revd Michael H. Eldon, first Bahamian Bishop of the Anglican Diocese of Nassau, The Bahamas and The Turks and Caicos and Dr Keva Bethel, first President of the College of The Bahamas, grew up there. Originally the house had an open porch which has been closed in. It was recently restored to house the International Travellers' Lodge.

# 23 Blue Hill Road

Also known as Baillou Hill Road after Isaac Baillou, an American Loyalist who owned land in this area, *Blue Hill Road* was opened in 1798. 'Blue Hill' is named after the range of hills in the area.

*St Agnes' Church*, Grant's Town, is located just south of the Southern Recreation Grounds and Archdeacon William Thompson's Softball park. The church was consecrated by Bishop Venables on 15 July, 1868. Later, in 1906, Bishop Wilfred B. Hornby consecrated a spacious chancel and 'our Lady's Chapel' in memory of Bishop Henry N. Churton who drowned in 1904. The church was renovated in the mid and late twentieth century. Archdeacon Thompson served as Rector at St Agnes for 32 years between 1967–99.

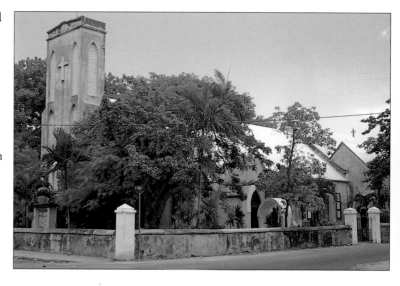

The *Grant's Town Post Office*, Blue Hill Road, was built in the Bahamian Colonial style around 1900. The second storey housed the original Grant's Town Library. The building was damaged during the 1942 riot and later restored. The Grant's Town Library evolved into the Southern Public Library which was established in 1951. The latter opened at new premises further north on Blue Hill Road. The late Dr Cleveland Eneas was one of the founding fathers of the *Southern Public Library*. Mrs Lillian Coakley served as Librarian for about 36 years.

*Cliff's Barbershop*, 104 Blue Hill Road, was built of stone in the early 1900s. This building once served as the United Burial Society Lodge Hall. Old timers congregate here to play checkers and the West African game of Warri.

*Sir Orville Turnquest's Birthplace*, Hay Street and Blue Hill Road. The fifth Bahamian Governor General in an independent Bahamas, Sir Orville Turnquest was born in a house on the site of the house pictured. The latter was built around 1933. It was a two-storey traditional Bahamian timber building (clapboard) with dormer windows, fish-scale decorations and a small front porch. Regrettably, the house perished in a fire in 2001. Sir Orville's parents, Robert (a businessman) and Gwendolyn Turnquest had seven children.

The present *Wesley Methodist Church*, Blue Hill Road, was built in 1868 on the site of an earlier 'Wesley Chapel' (1839). Methodist Missionaries worked in Grant's Town among the ex-slaves, free blacks and Liberated Africans as early as 1833. Wesley was under the care of the West Chapel, Nassau Court, but in 1847, with a membership of 158, it became an autonomous society. The 1868 church was almost entirely destroyed by the hurricane of 1926. The church was reconstructed in 1929 and renovated extensively in the mid and late twentieth century.

# *24* Meeting Street

This street is called after the original name of 'Bethel Meeting House', now the Bethel Baptist Church.

The land on which *Bethel Baptist Church* stands was purchased by ex-slaves and Baptist leader, Prince Williams and his associates. Initially, they worshipped in a small wooden building but later a more permanent stone structure was built (Bethel Meeting House c.1835). The latter was destroyed in the hurricane of 1866. A grant made by the House of Assembly assisted in the rebuilding of the church. It was opened and dedicated by the Revd Robert Dunlop of 'The Kirk' on 10 March, 1869. The present mid-twentieth century structure contains part of the old church.

The *Bosfield House* on West Street, near to Meeting Street, was built in 1900 out of imported lumber from Jacksonville, by Frederick Bosfield, a printer at the *Nassau Guardian*. In 1901 Mr Bosfield married Agnes Byndloss and they lived in a newly constructed house which has an attic and porch with railings on the western side. It once had an outside kitchen. In early 2000, Mrs Olga Nash and her sister Ms Lillian Bosfield, (daughters of Frederick Bosfield), still lived there. In 1981 the Bosfield House was awarded a Bahamas National Trust certificate for preservation.

This two-storey stone building, *Odd Fellows Lodge Hall,* is believed to have been constructed in the late nineteenth century. The St Bartholomew Lodge meets there. Mr Robert William Turnquest, father of Sir Orville Turnquest, rented the downstairs of the building where he operated a grocery shop from the late 1920s until the mid 1960s. After his death in 1966, the Lodge took over the entire building.

*St John's Native Baptist Church* was established in 1835 by Prince Williams and his followers, who left the 'Bethel Meeting House' after a dispute arose. They congregated in various buildings until a stone building with a thatched roof was erected on the site of the present church. St John's has been expanded and renovated many times since its early beginnings. The Revd Dr O.A. Pratt, pastor for the past 35 years, succeeded pastor Dr T.E. Donaldson.

# *25* Elizabeth Avenue

Originally known as Union Street, *Elizabeth Avenue* was renamed in honour of
Queen Elizabeth II who was crowned in 1953.

The former *Willie Brooks
Family home* was built in
the late nineteenth century.
Mr Brooks was one of the
number of merchants who
sold English woollen goods
during the 1920s and 1930s.

*43 Elizabeth Avenue* was
originally the home of
Mr and Mrs E.Hilton
Curry, the parents of
Mrs Daisy Leonora Brown
née Curry.  Daisy Curry married
Herbert William Brown at
Lyndhurst in June 1923.
This traditional Bahamian
Colonial style house was
built by Joseph Elias Dupuch
for Mr E.H. Curry in the
late nineteenth century.
The house remained in the
Curry and Brown families
for many years.  It now houses
the legal offices of attorneys
Knowles, McKay and Culmer.

# 26 Victoria Avenue

Named after Queen Victoria (1837– 1901), this avenue was planted with Royal Palms by the Queen Victoria Chapter of Daughters of the Empire in 1904. Some palms are still alive today.

*Zode House* was built of cut stone with a tiled ground floor porch, between 1898 and 1900, by Charles Menendez. The contractor was Harry Glinton. The upper storey verandahs were added later. This family home (once with an outside kitchen and iron-gated garage), was passed from Charles and Alice Menendez to Ormond and Katherine Curry (early 1920s) and later to their granddaughter Patricia Vouch (née Curry). The property was sold in 1995 to Zode Holdings Ltd, which restored and re-named the Curry homestead Zode House. It represents the first letters of the owners' daughters' names.

# 27 Dowdeswell Street

This street, named in honour of Governor Dowdeswell (1796–1802), was known as 'Middle Street', running as it does between parts of Bay and Shirley Streets.

Built in the mid to late 1870s, *Gaylords Restaurant* (formerly 'Villa Flora') was occupied by Thaddeus George Johnson and his wife Mary Seavour Higgs of Dunmore Town, who raised a large family there. Johnson, a religious man, attended and preached at the Gospel Hall, a Brethren Church. Gaylords, established in the 1990s, is part of a well-known chain of Indian restaurants that offers authentic Tandoori and Indian specialities. The property is being held in trust for William James Rees, grandson of the late Dora Agnes Johnson.

*International Tea House*, 10 Dowdeswell Street. This wooden clapboard house was built around 1880. It was constructed on a Family Island, probably Abaco, and brought to Nassau and reassembled. Henry Stuart conveyed it to Henry M. Lightbourn in 1881 and he sold it to George R. Sweeting in 1920. It was passed to Fannie Maud Sweeting in 1923, who sold it in 1946 to Marie G. Kemp. Mrs Kemp received a certificate from The Bahamas National Trust for preserving it. The property is now owned by Mrs Kemp's three grandchildren, Penelope A. Hogg, P. Andrew Kemp and Paul A. Kemp. Patrice Bain manages the 'Tea House'.

The *Smith Homestead*, built around 1890, was owned by John 'Jack' Smith, MBE, who was employed in the House of Assembly from 1914 to 1969 (33 years as Chief Clerk, 1936–1969). It is a two-storey house constructed of masonry and surrounded by porches with wooden balustrades and lattice. It now houses 'The Kid's Club', a specialized care centre for children with disabilities.

The *Duncombe Residence* was built by Gurth Stafford Duncombe in 1930, on property purchased from the Anglican church. Married to Kathleen Adderley in 1931, they became the parents of Ann Johnstone and Sonya Kelly, who grew up there. The two-storey house, built mainly of Abaco pine, has wooden floors and wrap-around porches. In April 1987 the property was sold to Alfa Investments Ltd, owned by Jeffrey and Freddie Albury. Gurth S. Duncombe died in 1988. The residence is now being used as the Quality Auto Sales administrative offices managed by Garth M. Thompson.

The *Carey Home*, constructed of Abaco pine, with sash windows, louvres and ornate woodwork (seldom seen today), was built in the late nineteenth century by Thaddeus Johnson Senior. It has been renovated several times and has undergone two main changes. A second storey eastern porch was enclosed to provide two additional bedrooms, and a large section of the rear of the house was removed and reassembled on the lot immediately to the west. The property was later purchased by brothers, Ormond and Willie Carey, who divided the building so that each could have a home. After the death of Ruby Carey-Mathers (Ormond's daughter and last in line of the Carey family), the house was purchased by Donald Russell (nephew). Cousin David Russell currently resides there.

The original *St Matthew's Rectory* dates from 1903– 5 and is located on Lovers Lane, just south of the present one on Dowdeswell Street. It later became St Peter's Convent and then reverted back to a Rectory before becoming the *Templeton Theological Seminary*. Renovations are in progress again for its use as a Youth Centre for St Matthew's Parish.

The current *St Matthew's Rectory*, opposite the Eastern Parade, dates from 1946. It was first occupied by Father Donald Knowles, a Bahamian, who later became Bishop of Antigua in 1963. Father James Palacious, Rector of St Matthew's, and his wife, Reverend Angela Palacious, the first woman to be ordained in the Anglican Church in The Bahamas, currently live there.

# 28 Fortifications and their environments

*Fort Montagu*, sits on the site of an earlier structure dating to c.1725. The present fort was built between 1741–2 by Peter Henry Bruce, an engineer, during the governorship of John Tinker (1738–58). It was built of locally-cut limestone and named after the Duke of Montagu. A sea battery, north-east of the fort was called Bladen's Battery after the Governor's son. Fort Montagu and Bladen's Battery mounted eight 18, three 9 and six 6 pounders. Originally, the fort contained a rain water cistern, barracks for officers and soldiers, a guardroom and powder magazine.

*Fort Charlotte*, named in honour of King George III's wife, really comprised three forts: Fort Charlotte, the eastern section, Fort Stanley, the middle section and Fort D'Arcy, the western section. The building of the forts, out of solid rock, was begun in 1787 and completed in 1819. A dry moat surrounds Fort Charlotte and is spanned by a wooden bridge on the north side. These forts never fired a gun in battle and are now tourist attractions. They were constructed during the governorship of Lord Dunmore.

Built of cut limestone in the early 1790s during Lord Dunmore's governorship (1787–96), *Fort Fincastle* was named after Dunmore's second title, Viscount Fincastle.  It is situated on Bennet's Hill, overlooking the city of Nassau, Hog Island (now Paradise Island) and the southern and eastern sections of New Providence.  It is built in the shape of a paddle-wheel steamer and originally mounted two 24 pounders, two 32 pounders, two 12 pounders and one Howitzer. It served as a lighthouse and subsequent signal station until the lighthouse on Hog Island was completed in 1817.

The *Water Tower* was built in 1928 on Bennet's Hill adjacent to Fort Fincastle and stands about 216 feet above sea level. The tower is 126 feet high and its main purpose was to maintain water pressure in the city of Nassau. It is possible to go by elevator or walk to the observation platform at the top of the tower, where the view of the island, harbour and nearby cays is quite spectacular.

The *Queen's Staircase* or '66 Steps', in Elizabeth Avenue South, was cut out of solid limestone rock and leads to Fort Fincastle and its environs. The staircase, probably constructed in the 1840s, was named in honour of Queen Victoria.

The *Potters Cay Battery* was built by Lord Dunmore between 1793–4. These ruins have been stabilized and can be visited. Lord Dunmore also had batteries erected at Fort Winton and Hog Island during this period.

Named after the notorious pirate Edward Teach, also known as 'Blackbeard', *Blackbeard's Tower* is said to have been used as a 'look-out' to the eastern approaches of New Providence harbour. It is not certain when the tower was constructed but some believe it was in the eighteenth century. According to a 1999 AP news release, circumstantial evidence is mounting that a shipwreck off the Atlantic coast is the pirate Blackbeard's flagship, the 'Queen Anne's Revenge', which sank in 1718. Blackbeard terrorized ships in the Caribbean, The Bahamas and the east coast of the USA in the early 1700s.

# 29 Nassau harbour

The *Nassau Lighthouse*, situated on Paradise Island (formerly Hog Island), was built between 1816–17 to assist mariners and boat captains in navigating the Nassau harbour. Other lighthouses 'hand-wound kerosene burning lightstations' were built by the Imperial Lighthouse Service later in the century, mainly in the 1830s, 60s and 70s.

*Cruise ships* in the harbour. Nassau's harbour is renowned as a popular port for numerous historic seafaring vessels and in recent years, major cruise line traffic.

*Bahamas Ironmongery Co. Ltd (Old Nassau)*, Woodes Rogers Walk. This building, located on the northern side of Bay Street, was built around 1886, the same year that the Young family established the Ironmongery Co. Ltd. on the southern side of Bay Street. The store primarily sold hardware, ship supplies and saddlery. The business remained family-owned and operated over the ensuing years under the ownership of Mr Gurth Duncombe followed by Mr Philip Pinder along with his brother Percival and two sons Edmond and Gurth.

*Ministry of Tourism Information Office*, Woodes Rogers Walk featuring an attraction from the 'Pirates of Nassau' museum.

*Statue to Bahamian Women*, Woodes Rogers Walk. This statue, erected in 1974 in honour of Bahamian women, was sculptured by the late Randolph Johnston, an American who made his home in Little Harbour, Abaco.

# *30* Paradise Island

*Paradise Island* was formerly known as Hog Island

Sun International, led by Mr Sol Kerzner, has transformed Paradise Island. The *Atlantis* development, built on 29 acres, includes a hotel, casino, marina, elegant dining venues, the world's largest marine habitat with 11 exhibit lagoons and a simulated exploration of the mythical Atlantis ruins. The new facilities were opened in December 1998 followed by a large convention centre in July, 1999. Pictured in the foreground of Atlantis is the former exclusive 'Porcupine Yacht Club' built in 1933, now the main restaurant of Club Mediterranee, on Paradise Island.

*Grayleath* was built around the 1920s by A.V. Davies, a wealthy American, who sold it in the 1940s to Mr and Mrs Walter Killam. The Killams, also Americans and owners of Graycliff from the late 1940s to early 1960s, divided their time between Graycliff and Grayleath – their 'cottage'. Grayleath, near the posh and exclusive Porcupine Club, had several features added, including two swimming pools (one Olympic size), during the Killam's ownership. Grayleath is now incorporated into Club Med on Paradise Island.

*The Cloister*, Paradise Island. This cloister with columned sides and arches, was built in the twelfth to thirteenth centuries at Montrejau, France by the Augustinian Order. It was brought to The Bahamas and rebuilt in 1962 by J. J. Castremanne (Architect J. L. Volk), as part of millionaire Huntington Hartford's initial development of the Paradise Island Resort.

*Two bridges*, built in 1967 and 1998, cross the harbour from New Providence to Paradise Island.

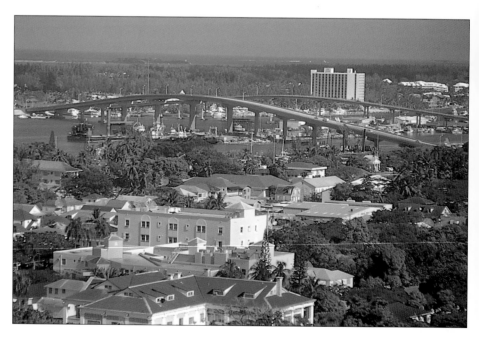

# 31 Oakes Field

The *College of The Bahamas* 'building' was completed in 1959 and the Government High School, formerly located in Nassau Court, moved there in 1960. The College of The Bahamas was established in 1974 and began operation during the following year. The College moved into the present building in 1976.

The *Nassau Guardian* newspaper, established on 23 November, 1844, is printed in this modern building. The newspaper was founded by Edwin Charles Moseley. Mary Moseley, granddaughter of the founder and first editor of *The Nassau Guardian*, assumed the editor's chair in 1904 – a position she held for 48 years. In 1952 *The Guardian* passed out of the Moseley family when it was sold to a group of Nassau businessmen. In the late 1960s it was purchased by Mr and Mrs John Perry Jr, owners of *The Nassau Guardian* at the present time.

*The Harry Oakes Monument.* Mr, later Sir Harry Oakes came to The Bahamas in 1934. Born in Maine, Oakes discovered the Lake Shore Gold Mine in Ontario, Canada in 1914 and became a very wealthy man. He built a golf course on Cable Beach and developed the first aerodrome in The Bahamas known as Oakes Field. He also bought the New Colonial Hotel and re-christened it the British Colonial. Over a thousand labourers were employed on his projects. Harry Oakes served as a member of the House of Assembly and the Legislative Council and received a baronetcy in 1939. His mysterious murder in 1943 has never been solved.

# 32 Outskirts and Fox Hill

Father Frederick Frey established St Augustine's College (SAC) in 1945 and founded *St Augustine's Monastery* in 1946. Beginning on 4 January, 1945, classes conducted by Benedictine monks, were held in a small two-storey house known as the 'Niche' on the Roman Catholic Priory Grounds on West Street. The school later moved to Fox Hill where the cornerstone of St Augustine's College and Monastery was laid by the late Bishop Stephen A. Donahue, on 11 July, 1946. Monsignor John Hawes (Father Jerome), renowned architect-priest, designed the buildings. After finishing the monastery, Father Jerome retired to Cat Island where he had built (early 1940s) 'The Hermitage' on Mount Alvernia, the highest hill in The Bahamas. He died on 25 June, 1956.

*The Retreat*, on Village Road, is the headquarters of The Bahamas National Trust. The original part of the building dates to the late 1860s. The Retreat sits on an eleven-acre estate once owned by Arthur and Margaret Langlois, who between them collected some of the rarest palms in the world. The Bahamas National Trust also inherited the Langlois' worldwide seashell collection. Tours are conducted through the gardens daily.

The present *St Anne's Church,* built in 1849, is on the site of an earlier small wooden structure erected in 1740. The church was built to serve the settlement of Fox Hill and 'The Creek' also known as 'New Guinea'. In 1954 Canon David John Harold Pugh, was installed as priest-in-charge of the Parish Church of St Anne, Fox Hill, where he served for 41 years until his retirement. During his Rectorship, Father Pugh was instrumental in the church building's expansion and land acquisition for the construction of St Anne's School and environs. Father Pugh was made a Canon of the Cathedral in 1974. His successor is Father Crosley Walkine.

*St Anselm's Roman Catholic Church* was built in the early 1930s to serve the people of Fox Hill and Sandilands Village. Soon after St Anselm's consecration in 1934, a school, operated by the Sisters of Charity, was started. The Revd Father Bonaventure Hansen was St Anselm's first Benedictine pastor. Since then, other pastors at St Anselm's include the late Father Marcian Peters, Father Frederick Frey, founder of St Augustine's Monastery, Father George Wolf, Bishop Leonard Hagarty, and Father Pat Holmes. St Anselm's present pastor is Monsignor Preston Moss.

# 33 Gambier and Adelaide

*St Peter's Native Baptist Church* was built around 1880, to serve the people of Gambier Village, which was settled by Liberated Africans in the 1830s and by some of the freed mutineers from the US Brig 'Creole' in 1841. Gambier was established by Governor Sir James Carmichael Smyth (1829–31). Other free black settlements outside the town of Nassau included Carmichael and Adelaide in the south-west, Grant's Town and Bain Town just south of the city, Delancey Town just west of Nassau and Creek Village (new Guinea) and Fox Hill in the east.

Adelaide is 16 miles from Nassau and was named after William IV's Queen. The village, established by Governor Sir James Carmichael Smyth (1829–31), was settled in 1831 by Liberated Africans from the Portuguese vessel *Rosa*, captured by the Royal Navy. It is believed that the original *St James Church* was built around 1840. The church was originally built with limestone walls and a thatched roof. It has been renovated in modern times.

# 34 Clifton Point

These *cut-stone steps,* known as 'Pirate Steps', date back to about 1800 after the era of piracy had passed. They are located at the western end of New Providence (near Clifton) and were most likely carved during the Loyalist plantation era.

Pictured are some of the *Wylly Plantation ruins* located at Clifton. William Wylly, a Loyalist, arrived in The Bahamas after the American War of Independence. He was appointed Attorney-General in 1799 and had three plantations in New Providence, namely Clifton, Tusculum and Waterloo. Most of his 67 slaves lived and worked at Clifton, the largest plantation. Clifton comprised a Great House and adjoining buildings, slave quarters and several other structures. Wylly purchased the Clifton estate in the early 1800s and lived there between 1815–21. Recent archaeological research demonstrated that the rich historical evidence which has emerged is suggestive of Pre-Loyalist habitation in the mid-eighteenth century. Archaeological excavations have revealed much about the daily life of the master and his slaves and have added greatly to the documentary evidence. Lucayan artifacts have also been excavated there.

# Bibliography

Adams, H.S., 'Nassau's Architectural Appeal', *Nassau Magazine*, February 1938, V, No. 3.

Albury, Paul, *The Story of The Bahamas*, London and Basingstoke, 1975.

Bacon, E.M., *Notes on Nassau*, London, 1869.

Bruce, Peter H., *Memoirs of Peter Henry Bruce*, London, 1782.

Craton, Michael, *A History of The Bahamas*, London, 1962 (revised and reprinted 1986).

Craton, Michael and Saunders, Gail, *Islanders in the Stream, A History of The Bahamian People*, 1992 (Vol. I) and 1998 (Vol. 2), Georgia, University Press, Athens, Georgia.

Development Board, Nassau, Bahamas, *Historic Forts of Nassau in The Bahamas*, Nassau, 1952.

Douglas, Robert, *Island Heritage*, Nassau, 1992.

Dupuch, Etienne Jr. Publications, *The Bahamas Handbook 1998*, 'The Street on the Hill', by Gordon Lomer, Nassau, 1997.

Finlayson, Iris E., *A History of St Matthews Anglican Church*, Nassau, 1989.

*Harper's New Monthly Magazine*, XIX, Nov. 1874.

Lomer, Gordon, 'High, Mighty trod West Hill Street', *The Bahamas Handbook, 1999*, Etienne Dupuch Jr. Publications, Nassau, 1998.

McKinnen, D., *A Tour Through the British West Indies in the Years 1802-1803, giving a particular account of the Bahama Islands*, London, 1804.

Moseley, Mary, *The Bahamas Handbook*, The Nassau Guardian, Nassau, 1926.

Moss, Valeria Moseley, (Ronald G. Lightbourn, ed.), *Reminiscing Memories of Old Nassau*, Nassau, 1999.

Northcroft, G.J.H., *Sketches of Summerland*, Nassau, 1900.

*Nassau Guardian*, Tercentary Number, 30 October, 1929.

Peters, Thelma, P., 'The American Loyalists and the Plantation Period in The Bahama Islands', Ph.D. Dissertation, University of Florida, 1960.

*Plan of Nassau 1788*. (Archives, Nassau and Nassau Public Library, Bahamas).

Public Records Office, Nassau, Bahamas, *A Selection of Historic Buildings of The Bahamas*. Government Printing Department, 1975.

Russell Seighbert, *Nassau Historic Buildings*, Bahamas National Trust, 1980.

Saunders, Gail, *Bahamian Loyalists and Their Slaves*, London and Basingstoke, 1983.

Saunders, Gail and Cartwright, Donald, *Historic Nassau*, London and Basingstoke, 1979.

Shoepf, J.D., *Travels in The Confederation 1783–1784*, Philadelphia, 1911.

Stark, J.H., *History of and Guide to the Bahama Islands,* New York, 1891.

The Bahamas Historical Society, *The Diary of the Physician from the United States Visiting the Island of New Providence, 1823–1824*, Nassau, 1968.

*The Bahamian Architect. A Quarterly Review of Architecture in The Bahamas*, Spring, 1995; Summer, 1995; Spring, 1996.

Williams, Patrice M., *Chronological Highlights in the History of The Bahamas 600–1900*, Nassau, 1999.

Wolfe, John, 'Nassau's Architectural Heritage', *Nassau Magazine*, Spring, 1949, I, 3.

# Index

601 Nightclub — 35
Addington House — 30
Adelaide — 11, 100
Annunciation Greek
    Orthodox Church — 74
Apsley House — 58
Archives, Department of — 15, 16
Assembly House — 4, 17
Atlantis Development — 95
Aurora Lodge Hall — 54

Bahamas Financial Centre — 31
Bahamas Historical Society — 32
Bahamas Ironmongery Co. Ltd — 93
Bahamas National Trust
    15, 16, 80, 84, 98
Bahamian Women, statue to — 94
Bain Town — 11
Balcony House — 3, 15, 60
Bank House: see Hillcrest
Bernard Sunley Building — 15
Best Ever (Mortimer's)
    Candy Kitchen — 48
Bethel Baptist Church — 80
Blackbeard's Tower — 91
Blackbeard's Well — 23
Bosfield House — 80
Bostwick and Bostwick Chambers — 64
British Colonial Hilton Hotel — 23
Buena Vista — 77
Butler, Sir Milo, house of — 35
    statue of — 18
Butler Residence — 61

C.A. Christie Real Estate — 62
Carey Home — 86
Carmichael — 11
Cascadilla — 47
Cellar Restaurant — 53
Cenotaph — 19
Central Bank — 59
Christ Church Cathedral — 5
Christopher Columbus, statue of — 41
Christofilis Villa — 76
Church of God — 50
Church of God of Prophecy — 50
Churchill Building — 21
Cliff's Barbershop — 79
Cloister, The — 96
Coin of the Realm — 53
College of The Bahamas — 14, 97
Collins House — 32
Colombian Emeralds — 25

Corner House — 10, 46
Cumberland House — 67
Curry House — 21

Dagbros — 76
Deanery, The — 68
Delancey Town — 10, 11
Devonshire House — 70
Diocesan Building — 24
Duncombe Residence — 85
Dunmore House (the Priory) — 4

East Hill House — 6, 40
Ebenezer Methodist Church — 33
Environmental Health, Ministry of — 69

Fendi — 27
Fort Charlotte — 4, 88
Fort Fincastle — 4, 89
Fort Montagu — 88
Fox Hill — 3, 11, 98-9
Frederick Street Steps — 55

Gambier — 11, 100
Gaol — 4
Gaylords Restaurant — 84
Georgeside — 64
Glenton-Newton House: see
    Princess House
Glenwood — 5
Government House — 4, 7, 41
Grant's Town — 11
Grant's Town Post Office — 78
Graycliff — 7, 42
Grayleath — 95
Green Shutters — 51
Gregory Arch — 7, 59

Harry Oakes Monument — 97
Hermitage, the — 4, 6, 38
H.G. Christie Ltd — 47
Hillcrest (Bank House) — 6, 40
Hillside Manor — 68

International House — 73
International Tea House — 84
International Travellers Lodge — 77
Island Shop, The — 25

Jacaranda — 6, 39
James Knowles' Law Office — 29
John Bull — 26

Kirk, the: see
    St Andrew's Presbyterian church
Knowles, McKay &
    Culmer Law Firm — 82

Lace House: *see* Malone House
Laurelhurst-By-The-Sea                  36
Lightbourn Building                     62
Lighthouse: *see* Nassau Lighthouse
Lynhurst House                          82

Magistrate's Court                    13, 51
Magna Carta Court                       29
Majestic Tours                          68
Malcolm (Marmaduke) House               57
Malone House                            52
Marlborough Antiques                    70
Marlborough Arms                        66
Masonic Building                        22
Media House                             48

Nassau Harbour                          93
Nassau Lighthouse                       92
Nassau Public Library                  4, 20

O'Donnell House                       10, 45
Oakes Field                           13, 97
Odd Fellows Lodge Hall                  81
Old Damianos House: *see*
    Apsley House
Old Fort                                28
Old Nassau: *see*
    Bahamas Ironmongery Co. Ltd
Old Prison                              49
Over-the Hill                       10-11, 14

Paradise Island                        95-6
Pink Pearl                              37
Pink-un                                 37
Pirate Steps                           101
Pirates of Nassau Museum                66
Police Headquarters
    (Police Barracks)                   49
Pompey Museum of Slavery
    and Emancipation                  15, 24
    *see also* Vendue House
Post Office Building                    15
Postern Gate                           8, 43
Potters Cay Battery                     91
Princess House                          65
Princess Margaret Hospital              31
Priory, the: *see* Dunmore House
Public Buildings                       4, 17

Queen Street, No. 28                    71
    No. 30                              72
    No. 44                              72
Queen's Staircase                       90

Ranora House                           9, 44
Red Roofs                               34
Rees Building                           57
Retreat, The                            98
Royal Bank House                         5
Royal Bank of Canada                    26
Royal Victoria Hotel                  12, 20

St Agnes' Church                        78
St Agnes' Rectory                       61
St Andrew's Presbyterian
    church (the Kirk)                  5, 56
St Anne's Anglican Chapel               11

St Anne's Church                        99
St Anselm's Roman
    Catholic Church                     99
St Augustine's College
    and Monastery                       98
St Francis Xavier Cathedral         7, 9, 74
St James' Church                       100
St John's Native Baptist Church         81
St Mary's Church                        75
St Matthew's Anglican Church          4, 33
St Matthew's Rectory                    87
St Peter's Native Baptist Church       100
Salem Union Baptist Church              51
Sandals Royal Bahamian Hotel            28
Sandilands Village                      11
Sir Orville Turnquest's Birthplace      79
Sisters of Charity Convent             9, 45
Small Cottage                           72
Smith Homestead                         85
Solomon's Mines                         27
Sunningridge                             9
Sunnyside                               38
Supreme Court Building                  19

Temple, The                             34
The Fold                              10, 46
The Nassau Guardian                  6, 7, 97
Thompson Residence                      61
Toogood's Studio                        36
Tourism Information Office,
    Ministry of                         94
Tradewinds Building                     14
Tribune Building                        32
Trinity Methodist Church              12, 56

Vendue House                      2, 5, 15, 24
Verandah House                          60
Victoria, Queen, statue of              18
Victoria Hall                           54
Villa Doyle                         8, 16, 43

Water Tower                             90
Wesley Methodist Church                 79
West Hill House                        8, 42
Woodes Rogers, statue of                23
Worrell House: *see*
    Laurelhurst-By-The-Sea
Wylly Plantation ruins                 101

Yamacraw House                          73

Zion Baptist Church                     30
Zode House                              83